A COLORING BOOK for ADULTS and CURIOUS CHILDREN

VINTAGE
TRAVEL POSTCARDS

Jodie Randisi

ISBN 978-0-9960533-5-8

EST. **COWCATCHER** 1992
PUBLICATIONS
HILTON HEAD, SC

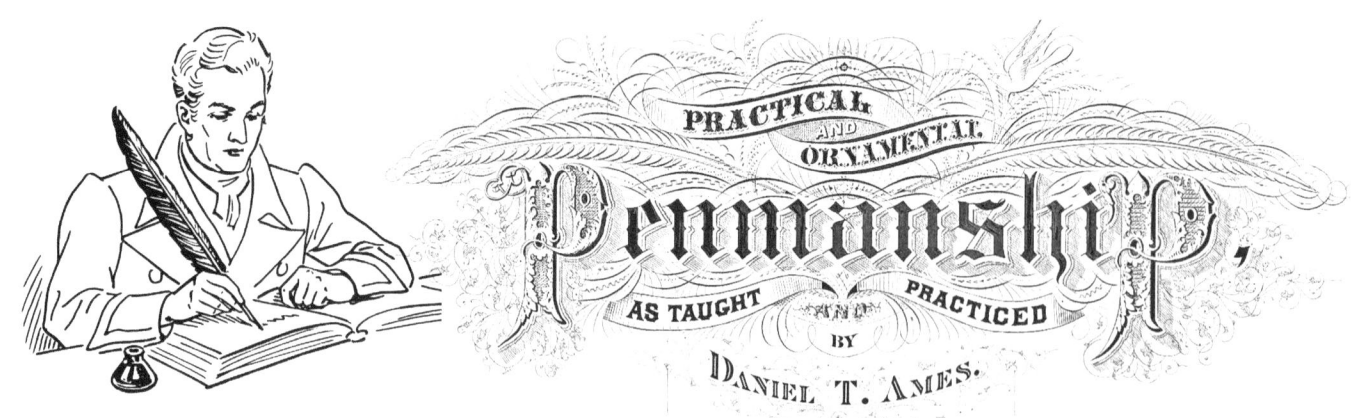

Copyright © 2016 by Jodie Randisi
All rights reserved.
Cowcatcher Publications
Vintage Travel Postcards Coloring Book
ISBN 978-0-9960533-5-8
Design by Steven Plummer, SPBookDesign.com
Graphics & illustrations, graphicsfairy.com, viintage.com, scrapgirls.com.

Post Card

PLACE STAMP HERE

HOW TO GET THE RESULTS YOU WANT

Best practices would be to remove pages from the book and make photocopies for the purposes of resizing and mistakes. Permission is given to make copies for your personal use only. Copyright restriction prohibits reproduction for commercial use. No permission is given to share, sell, or disseminate these pages without written permission from the publisher.

If you choose to color with markers, please be aware of problems with ink bleeding through the paper.

When you want to create a homemade postcard, make a copy on white cardstock paper. Extra postage will be charge if your postcard exceeds postal regulations.

To qualify for the postcard mailing rate, you must adhere to
At least 3½" high by 5" long, no more than 4¼" high by 6" long.

CHOOSE YOUR DESTINATION.

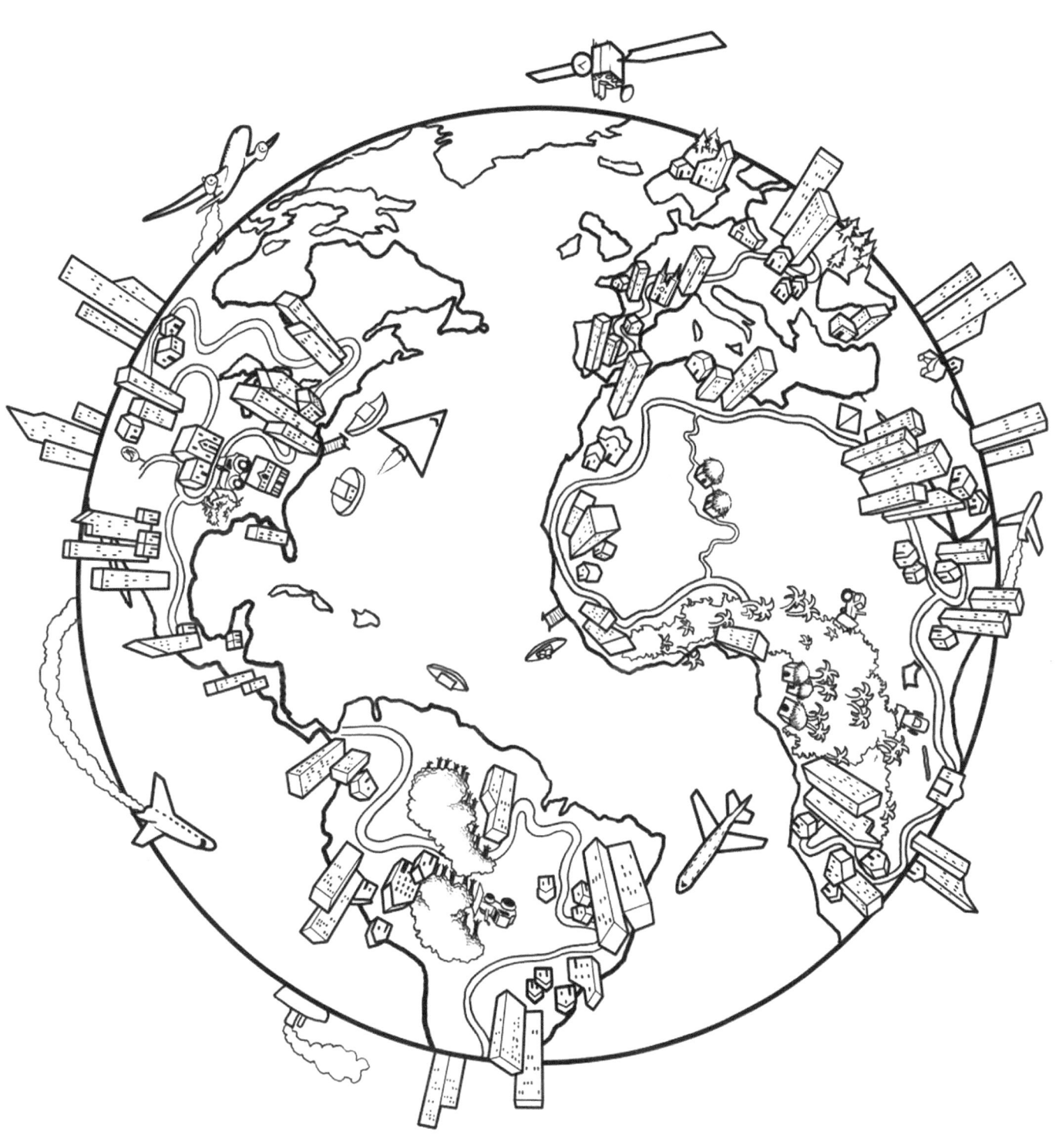

DON'T FORGET TO WRITE HOME.

Example

POST CARD

PLACE STAMP HERE

POST CARD

PLACE STAMP HERE

For fishing...
in a setting
of flowers
and music...
MEXICO
VERACRUZ
DEPARTAMENTO DE TURISMO DE LA SECRETARIA DE GOBERNACION

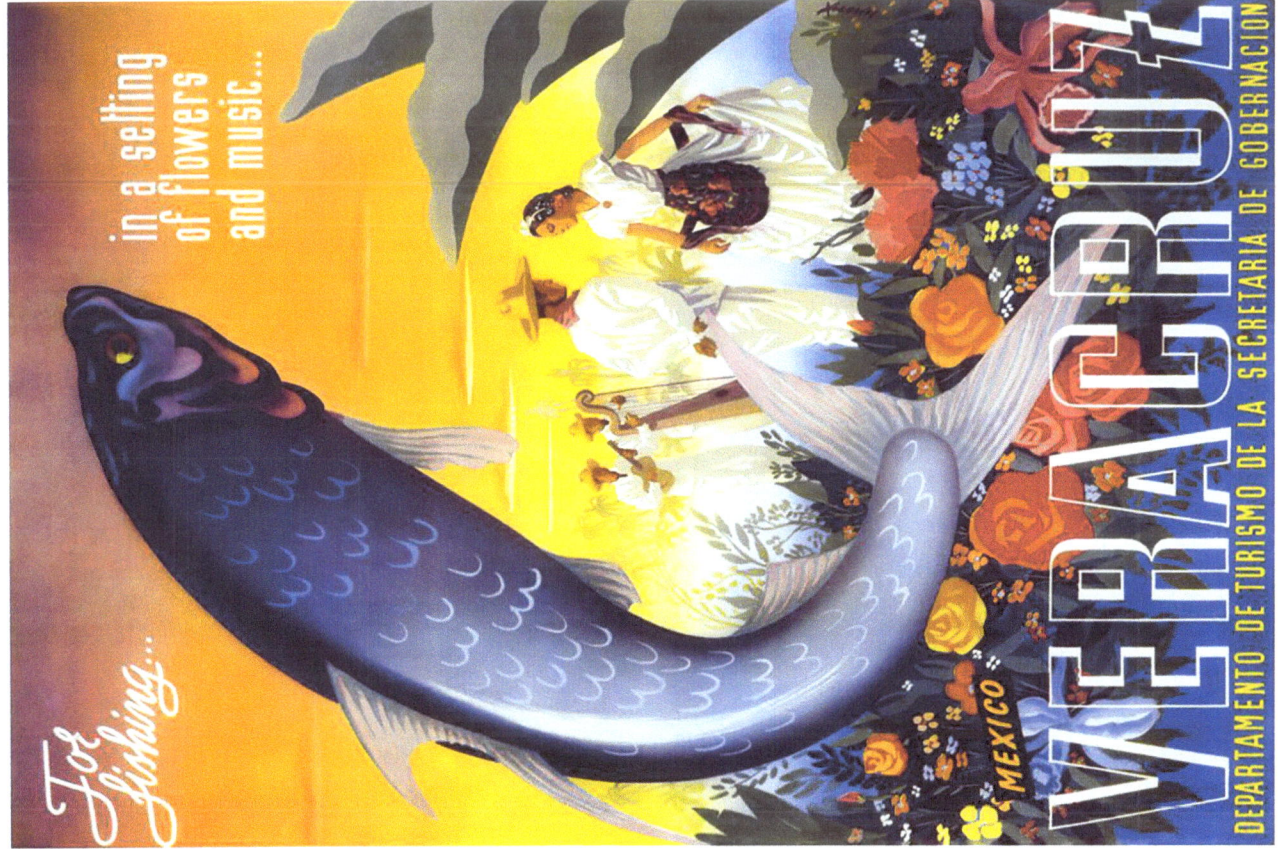

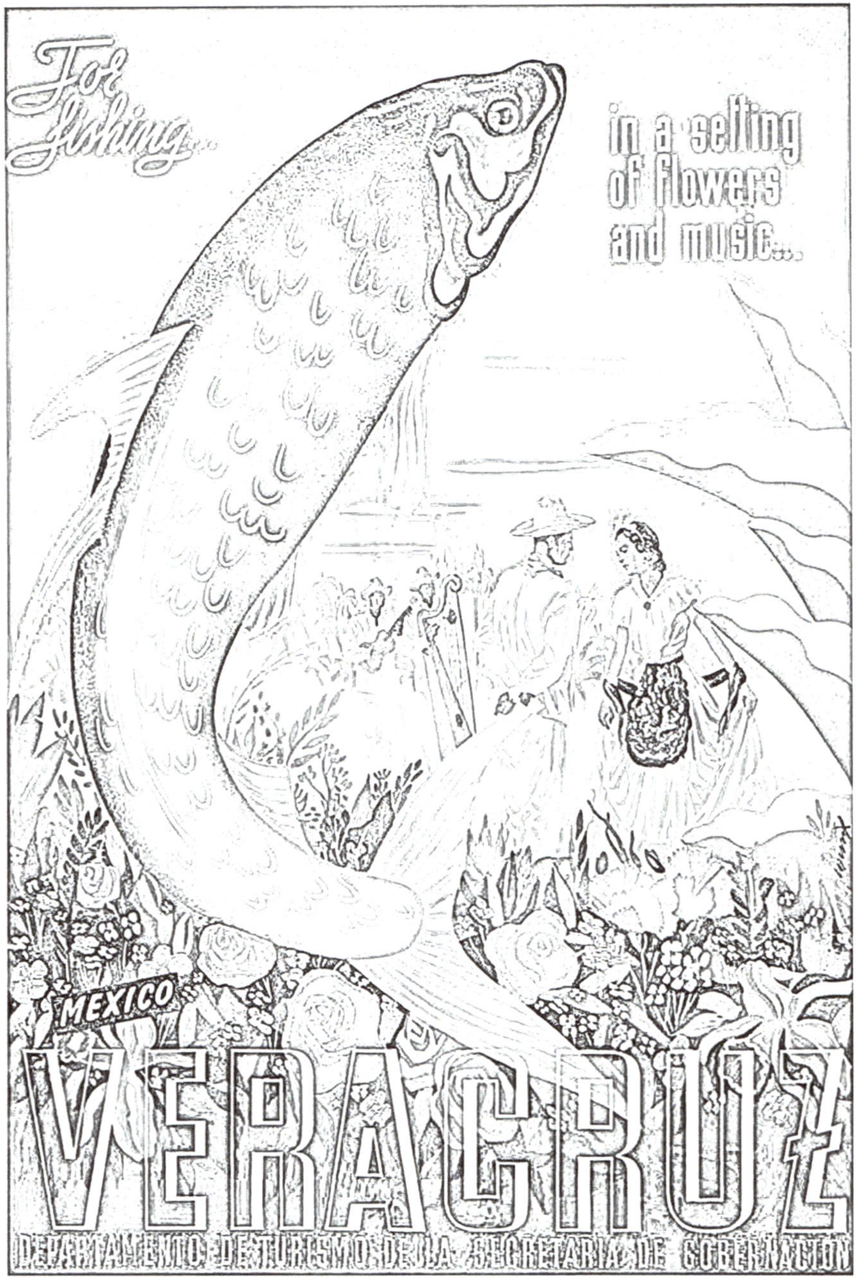
For fishing...
in a setting
of flowers
and music...
MEXICO
VERACRUZ
DEPARTAMENTO DE TURISMO DE LA SECRETARIA DE GOBERNACION

POST CARD

PLACE STAMP HERE

POST CARD

PLACE STAMP HERE

VITTORIO GRASSI
E.N.I.T.
VENISE ET LE LIDO
FS
ITALIE

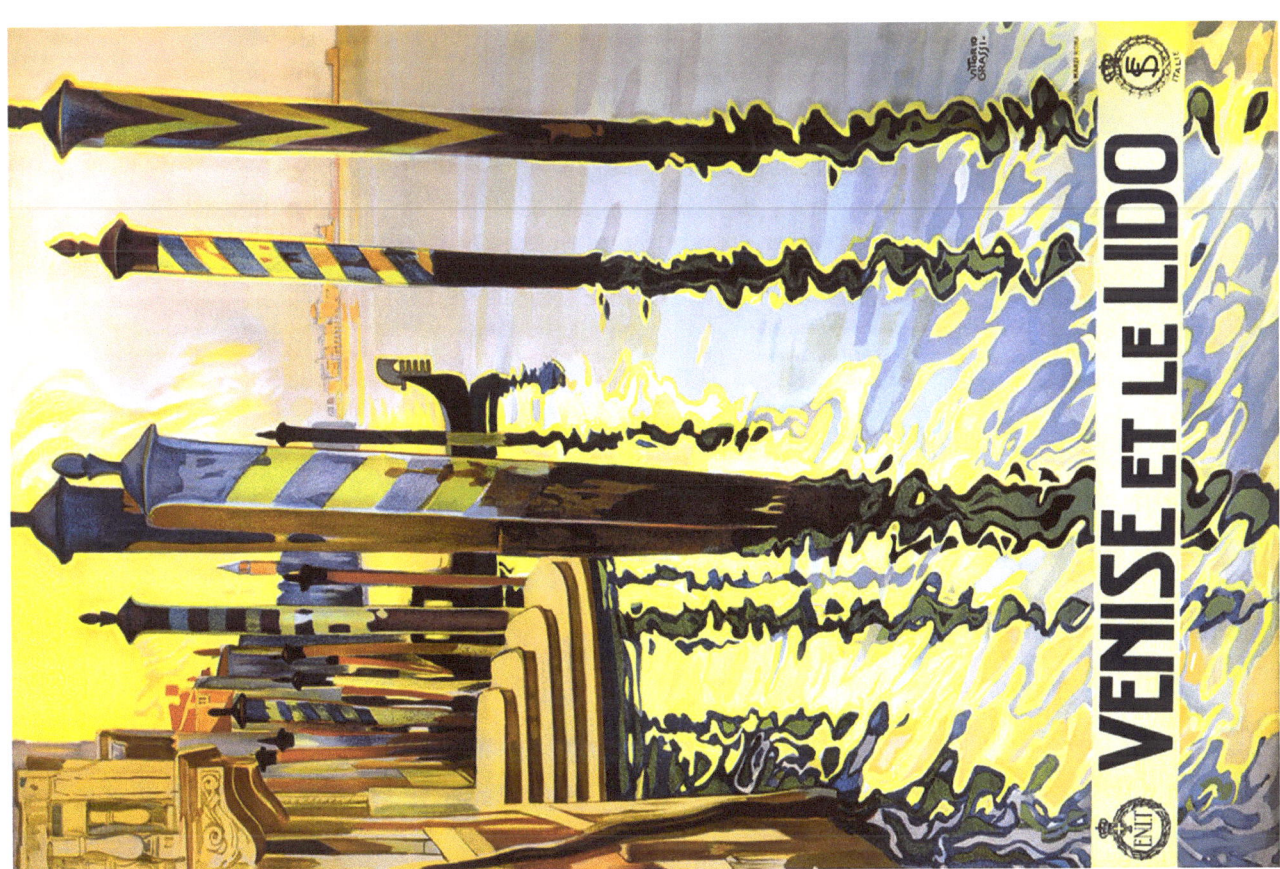

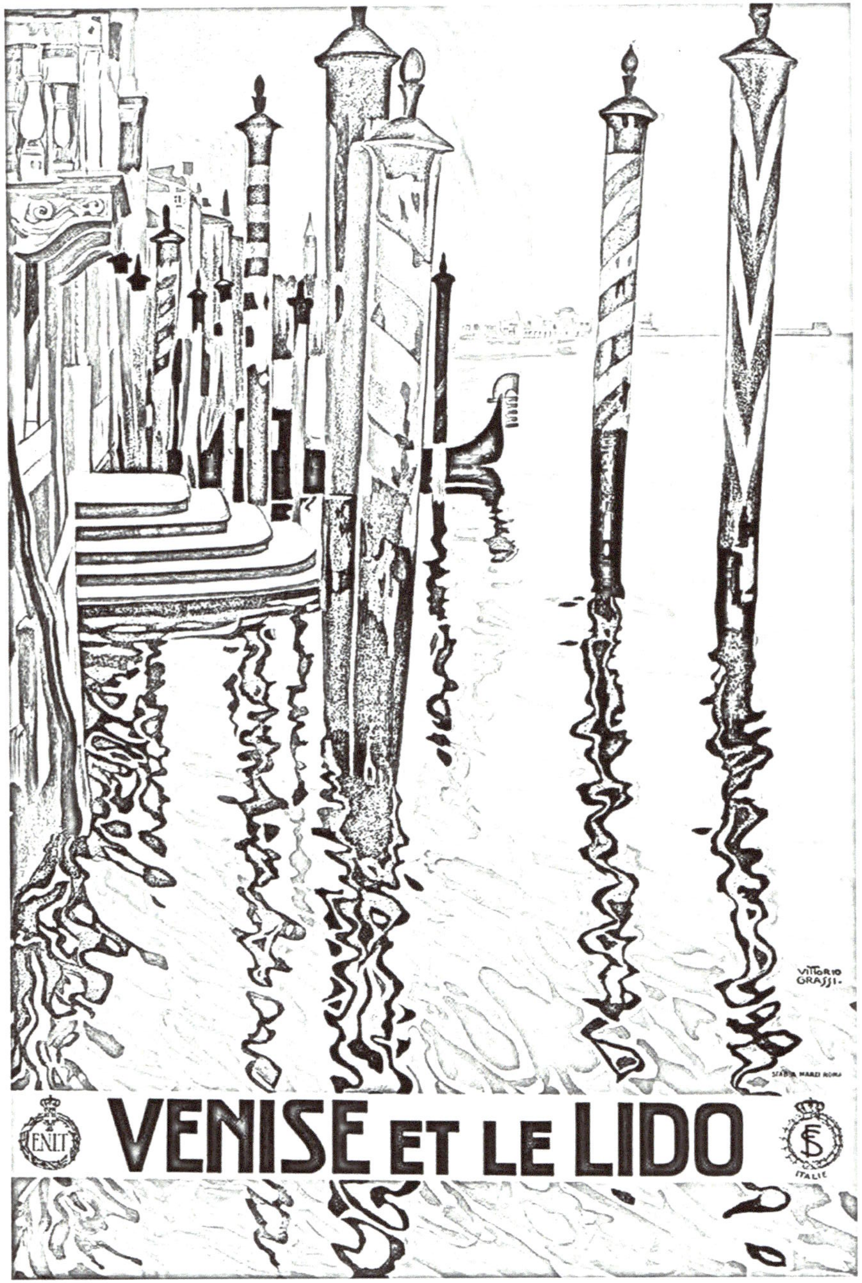
VITTORIO GRASSI
E.N.I.T.
VENISE ET LE LIDO
FS
ITALIE

POST CARD

PLACE STAMP HERE

POST CARD

PLACE STAMP HERE

POST CARD

PLACE STAMP HERE

POST CARD

PLACE STAMP HERE

fly to the
CARIBBEAN
by Clipper
PAN AMERICAN WORLD AIRWAYS
The System of the Flying Clippers

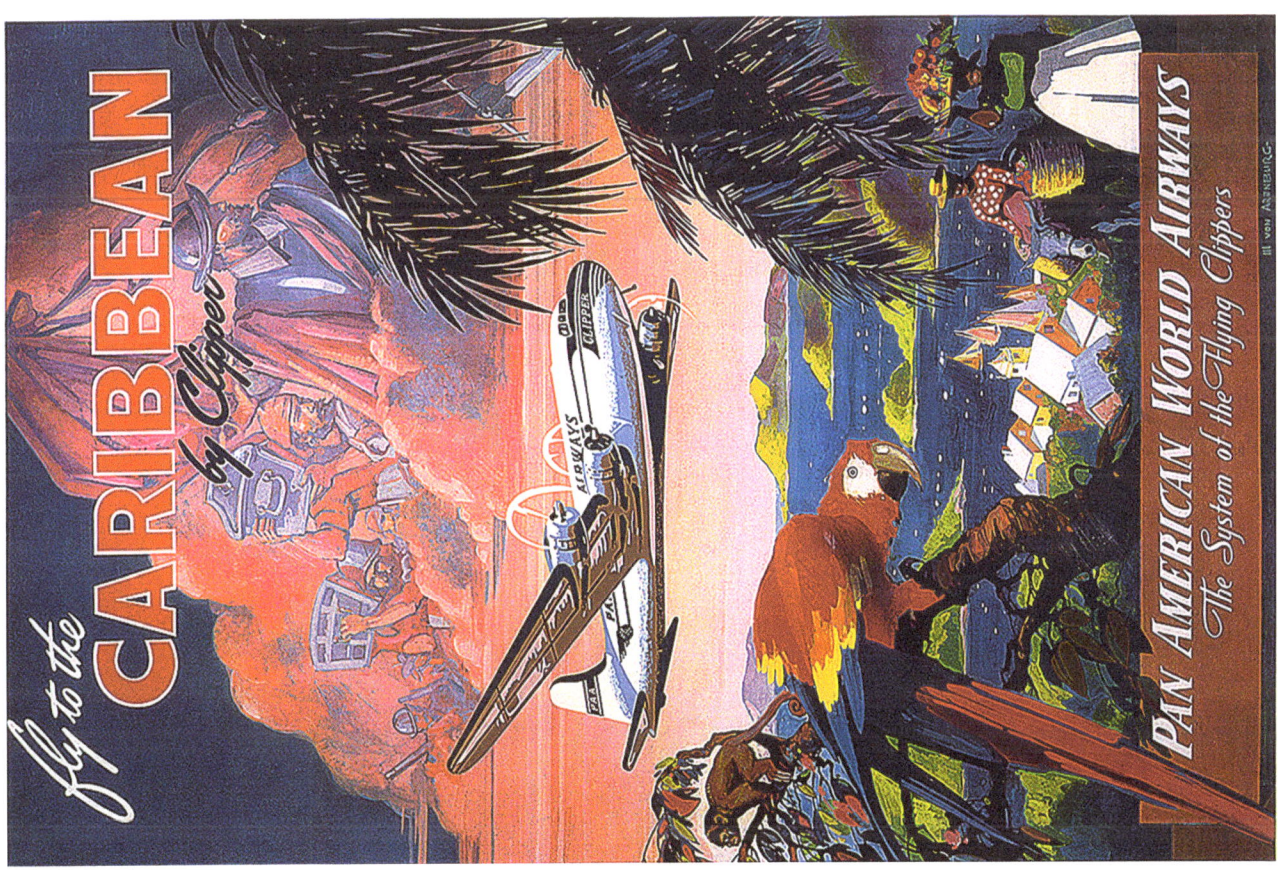

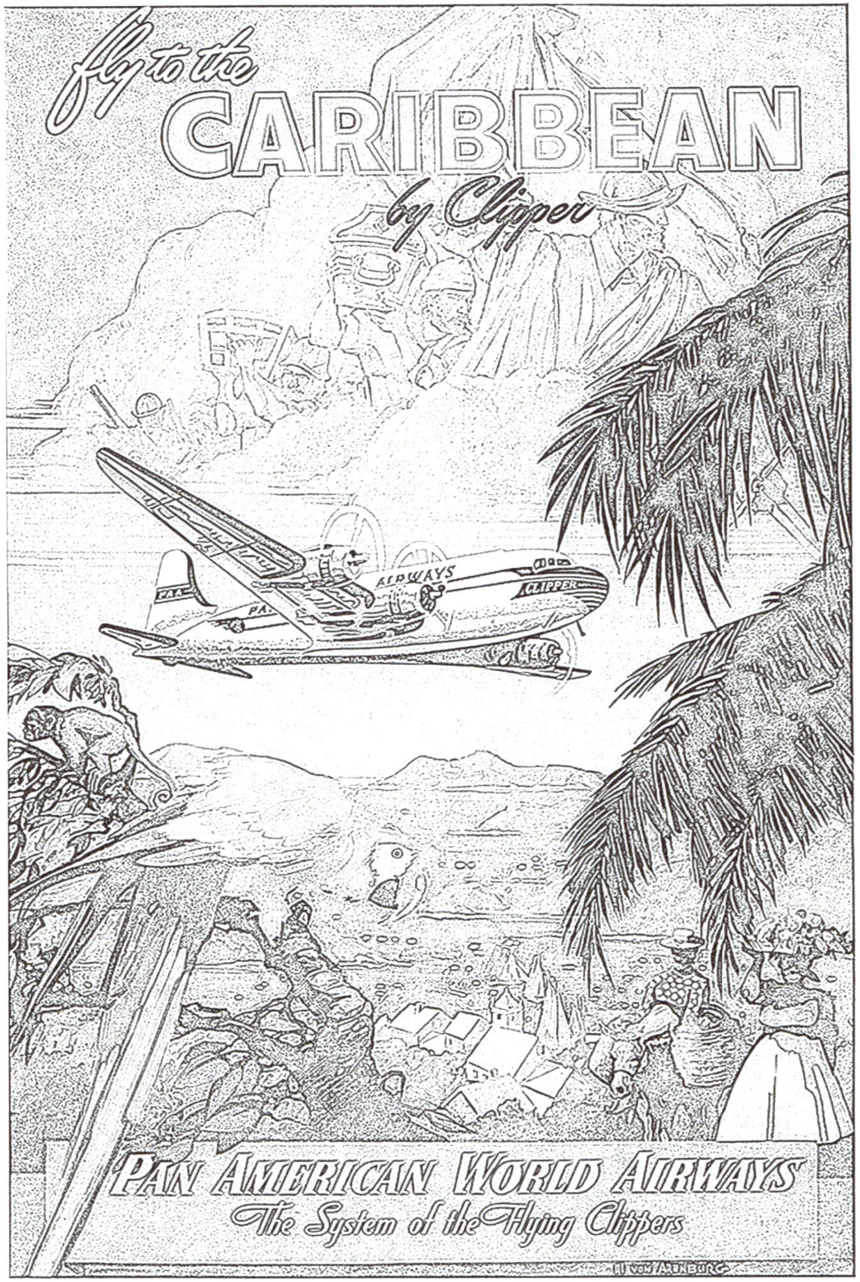
fly to the
CARIBBEAN
by Clipper
PAN AMERICAN WORLD AIRWAYS
The System of the Flying Clippers

POST CARD

PLACE STAMP HERE

POST CARD

PLACE STAMP HERE

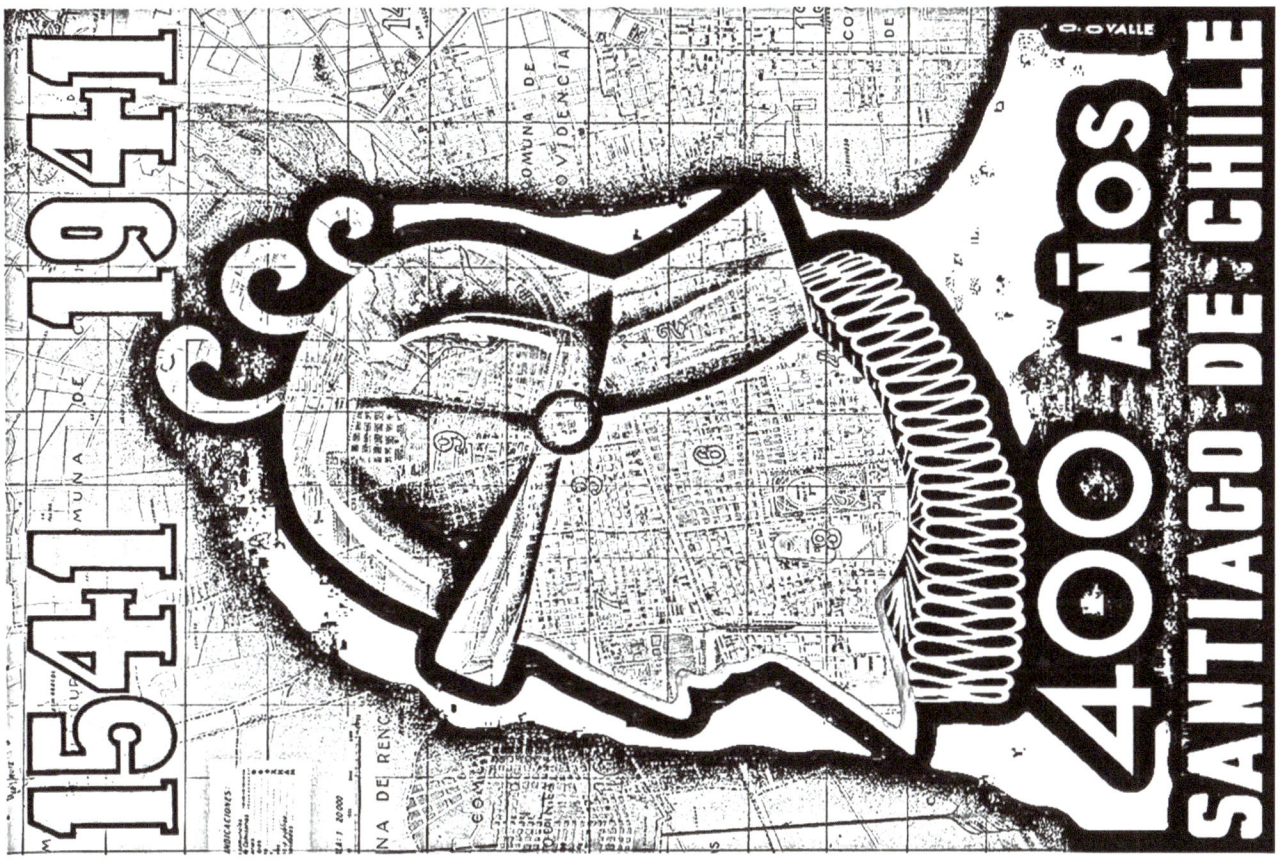
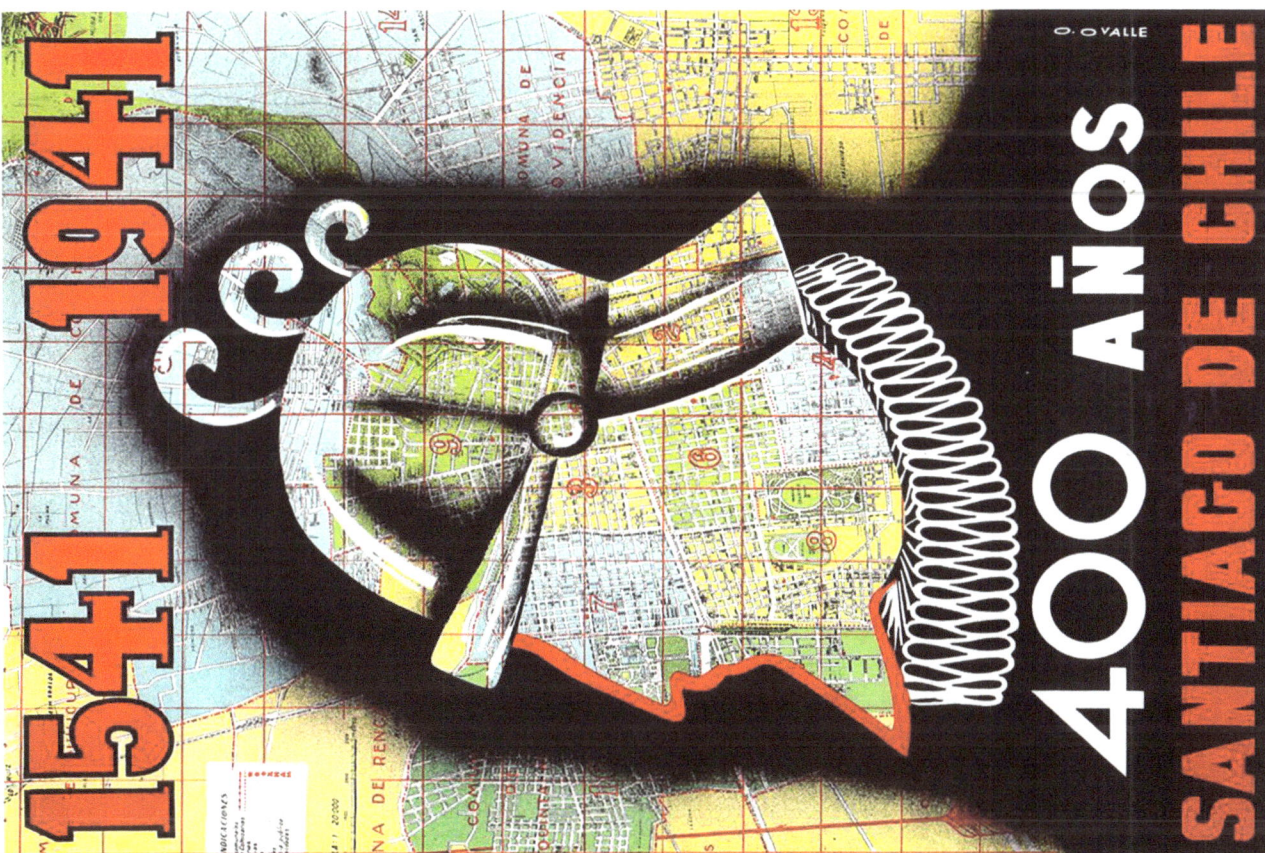

POST CARD

PLACE STAMP HERE

POST CARD

PLACE STAMP HERE

POST CARD

PLACE STAMP HERE

POST CARD

PLACE STAMP HERE

VISIT
CUBA
MAS SAG UER

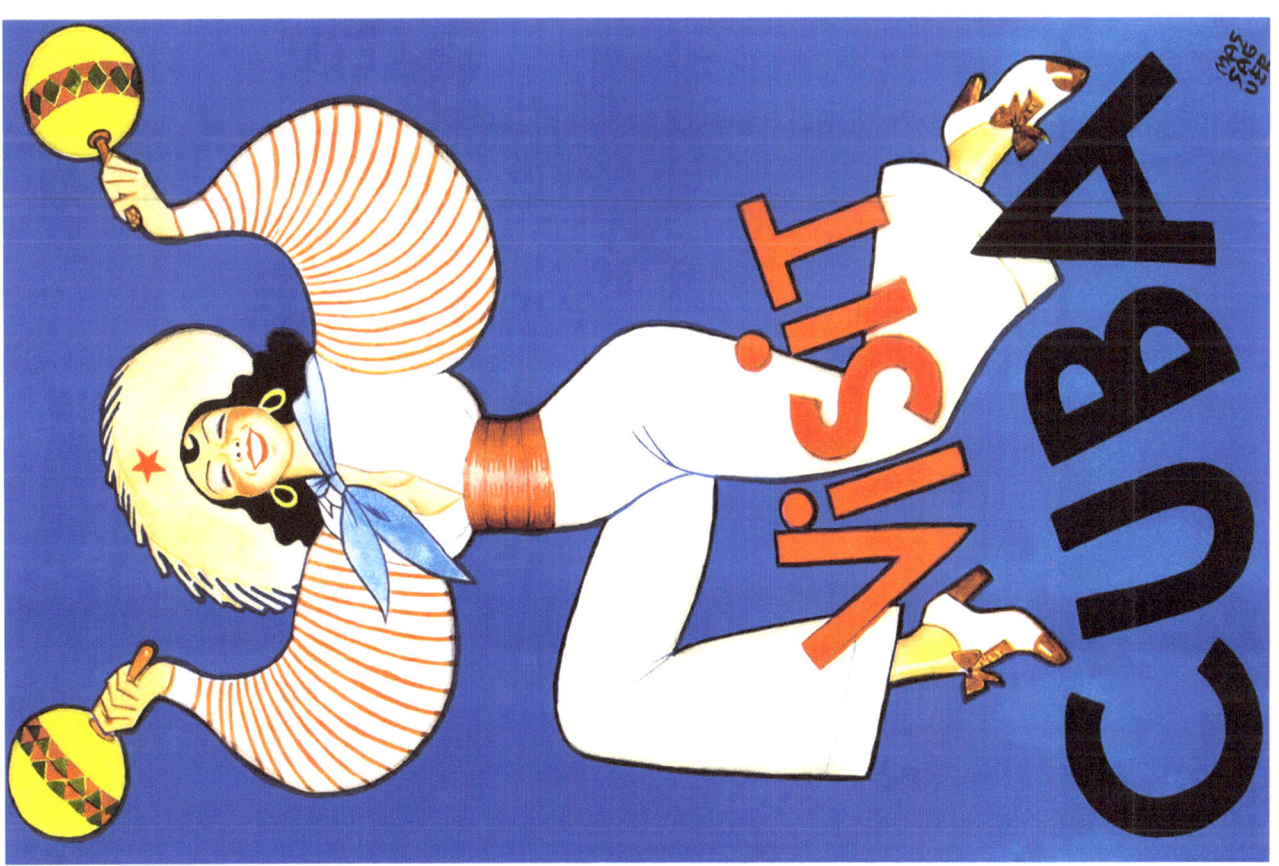

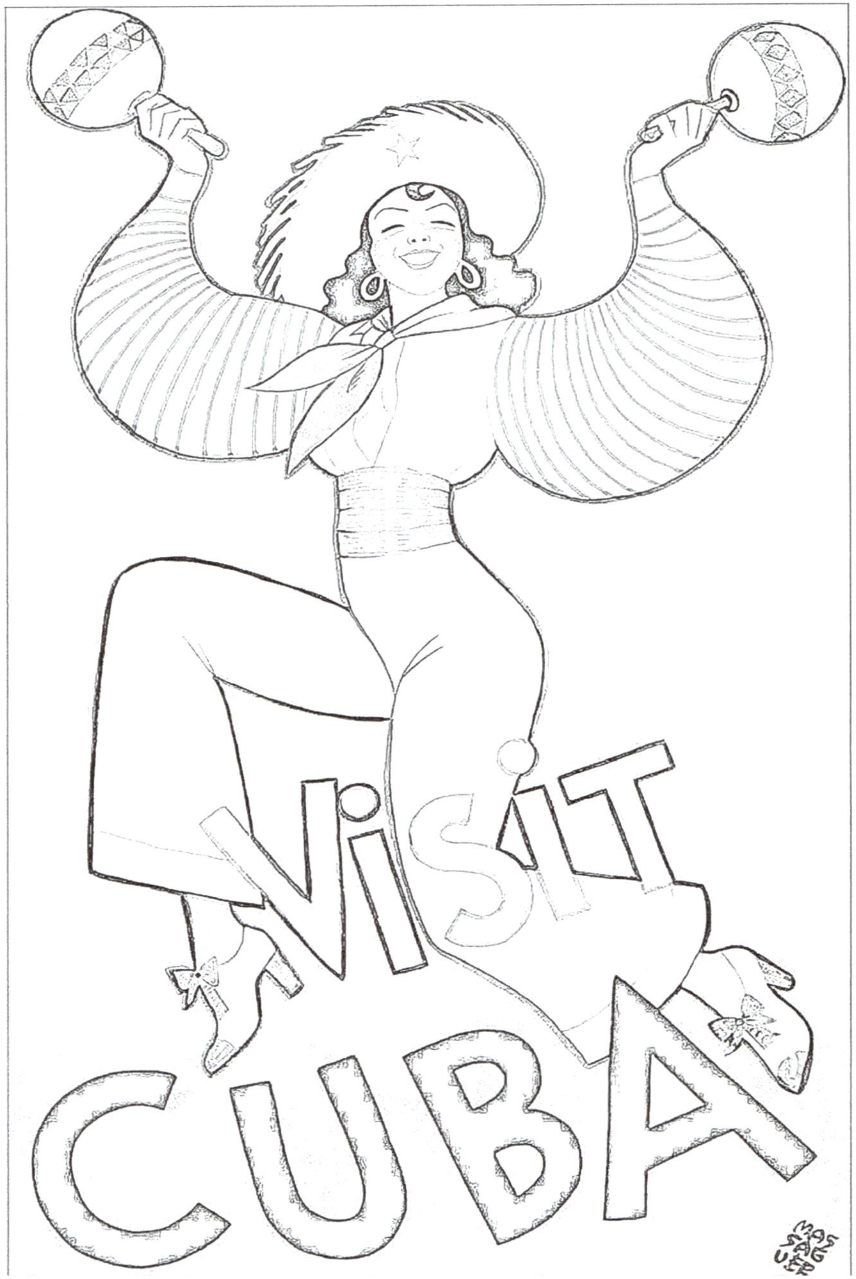
VISIT
CUBA
MAS SAG UER

POST CARD

PLACE STAMP HERE

POST CARD

PLACE STAMP HERE

POST CARD

PLACE STAMP HERE

POST CARD

PLACE STAMP HERE

POST CARD

PLACE STAMP HERE

POST CARD

PLACE STAMP HERE

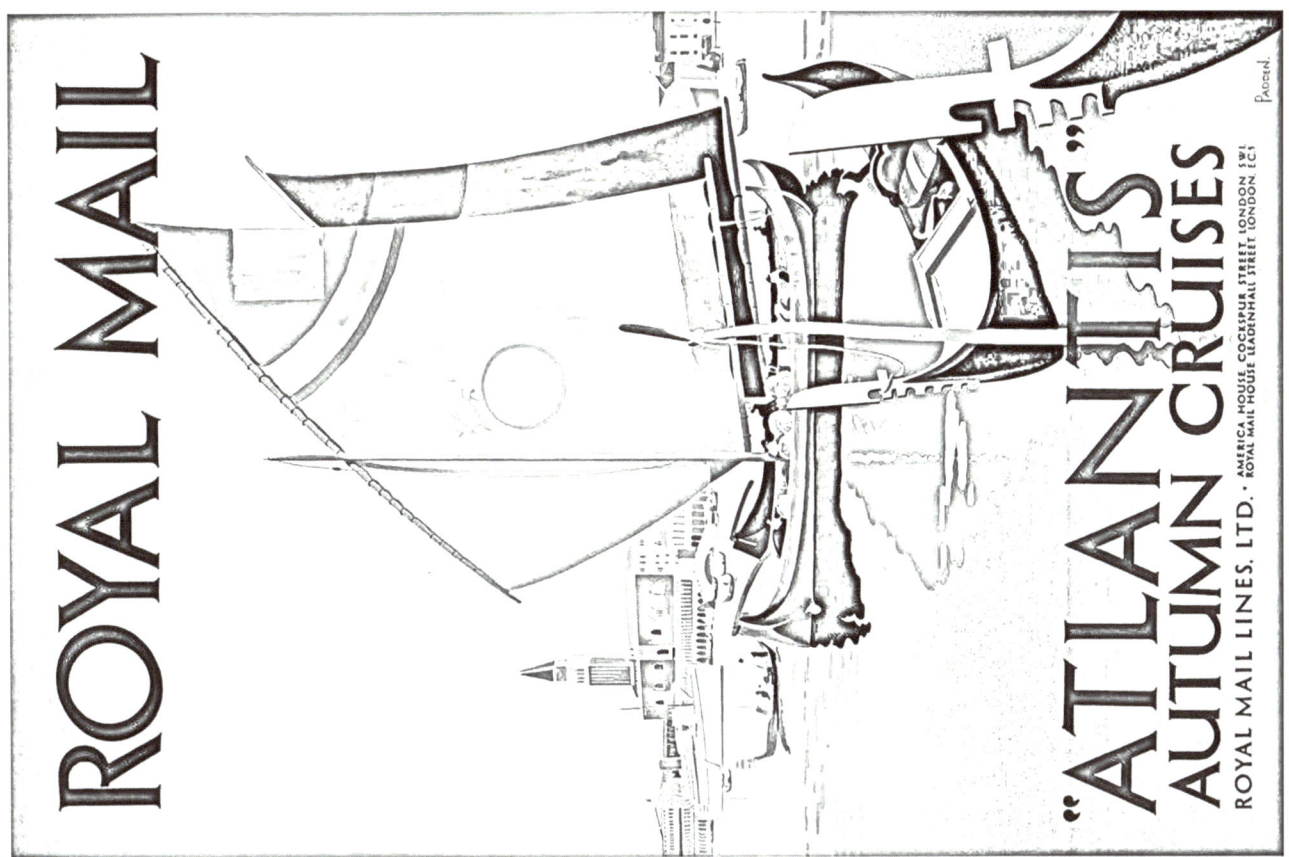

POST CARD

PLACE STAMP HERE

POST CARD

PLACE STAMP HERE

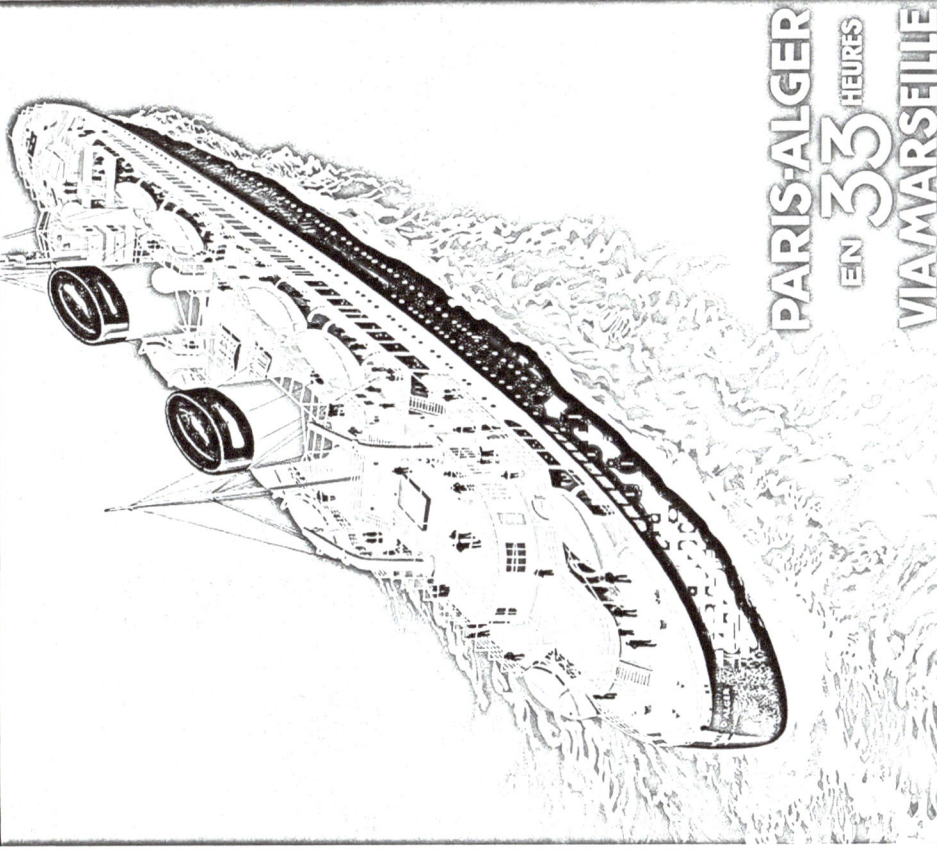

POST CARD

PLACE STAMP HERE

POST CARD

PLACE STAMP HERE

MEXICO
DIRECCION GENERAL DE TURISMO
JUAREZ No. 89
MEXICO 1, D. F.

MEXICO
DIRECCION GENERAL DE TURISMO
JUAREZ No. 89
MEXICO 1, D. F.

POST CARD

PLACE STAMP HERE

POST CARD

PLACE STAMP HERE

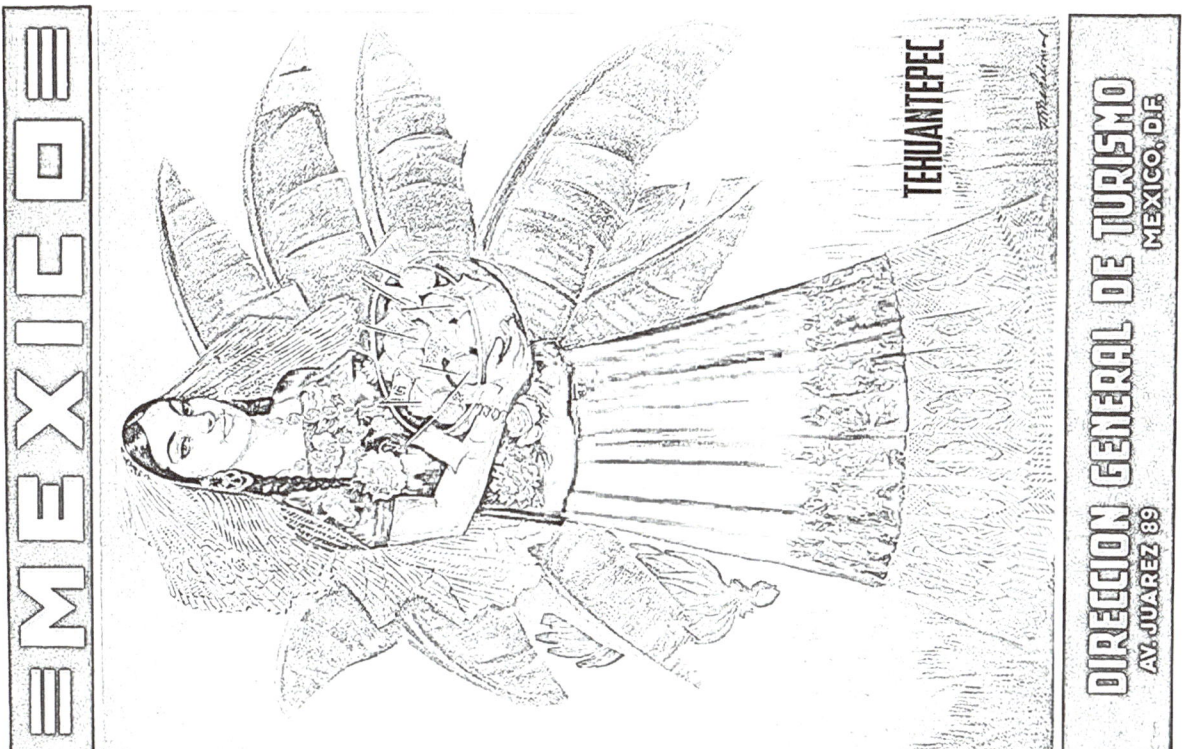

POST CARD

PLACE STAMP HERE

POST CARD

PLACE STAMP HERE

miami
HOYT
BRANIFF International AIRWAYS

miami
HOYT
BRANIFF International AIRWAYS

POST CARD

PLACE STAMP HERE

POST CARD

PLACE STAMP HERE

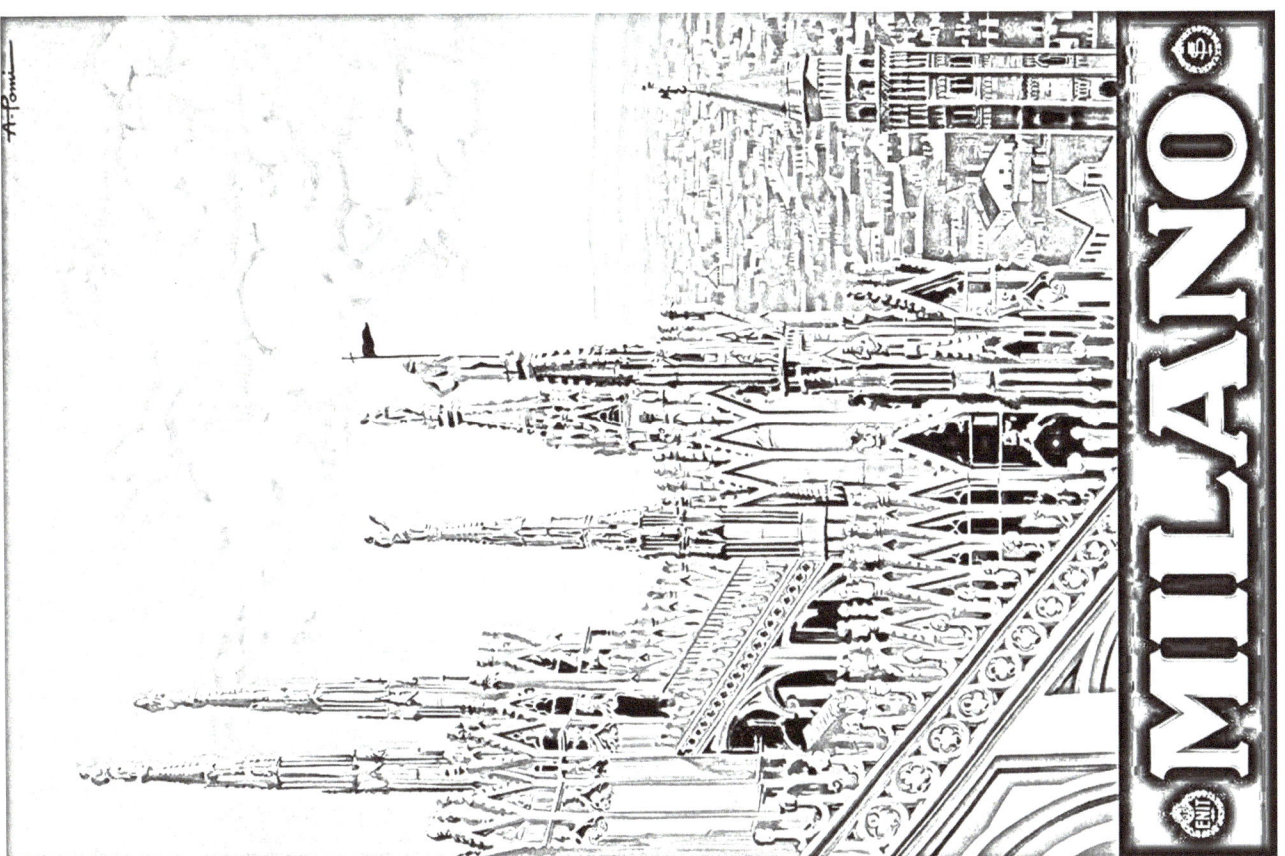

POST CARD

PLACE STAMP HERE

POST CARD

PLACE STAMP HERE

POST CARD

PLACE STAMP HERE

POST CARD

PLACE STAMP HERE

New Mexico
and
Arizona
Rockies
Land of
History
and
Mystery
Travel by Train
THE WILMARTHS

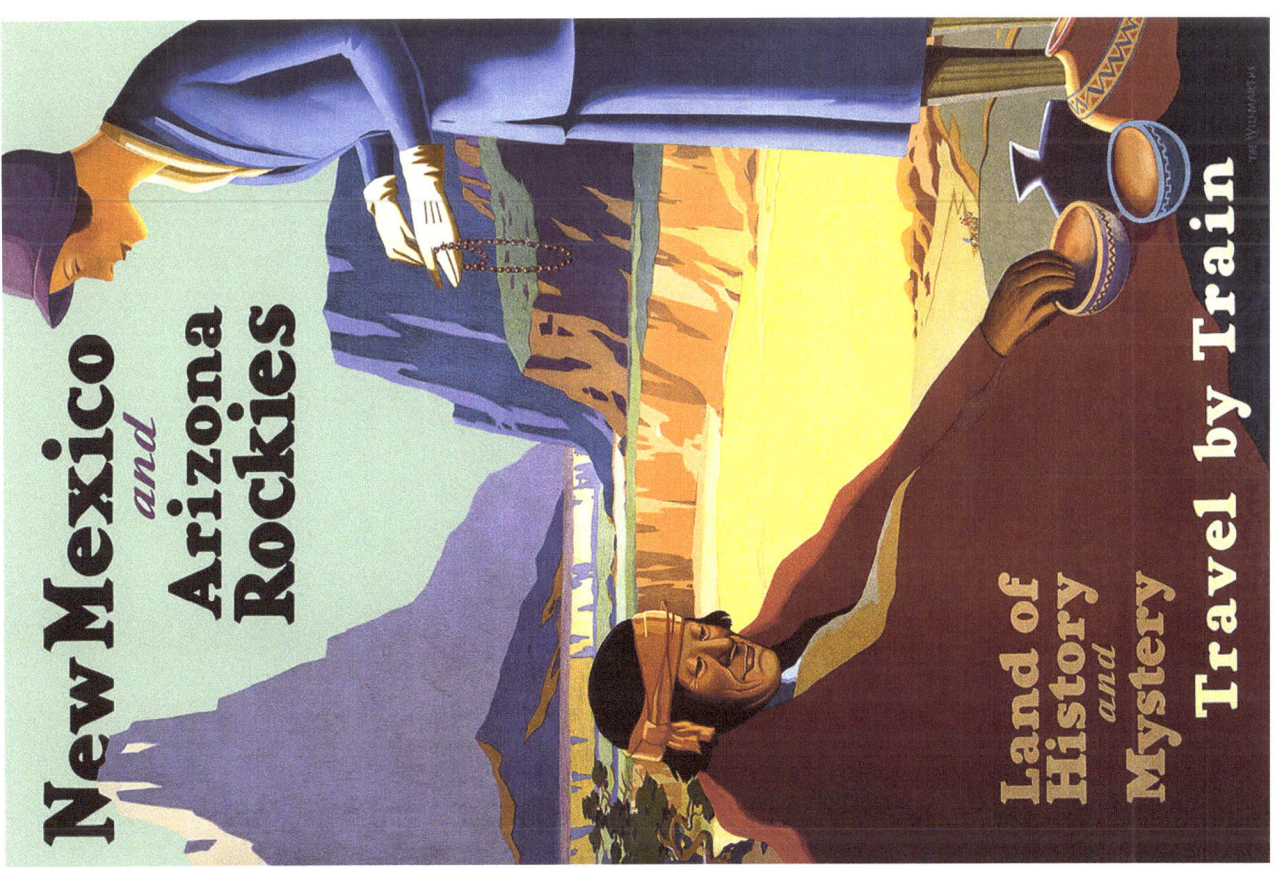

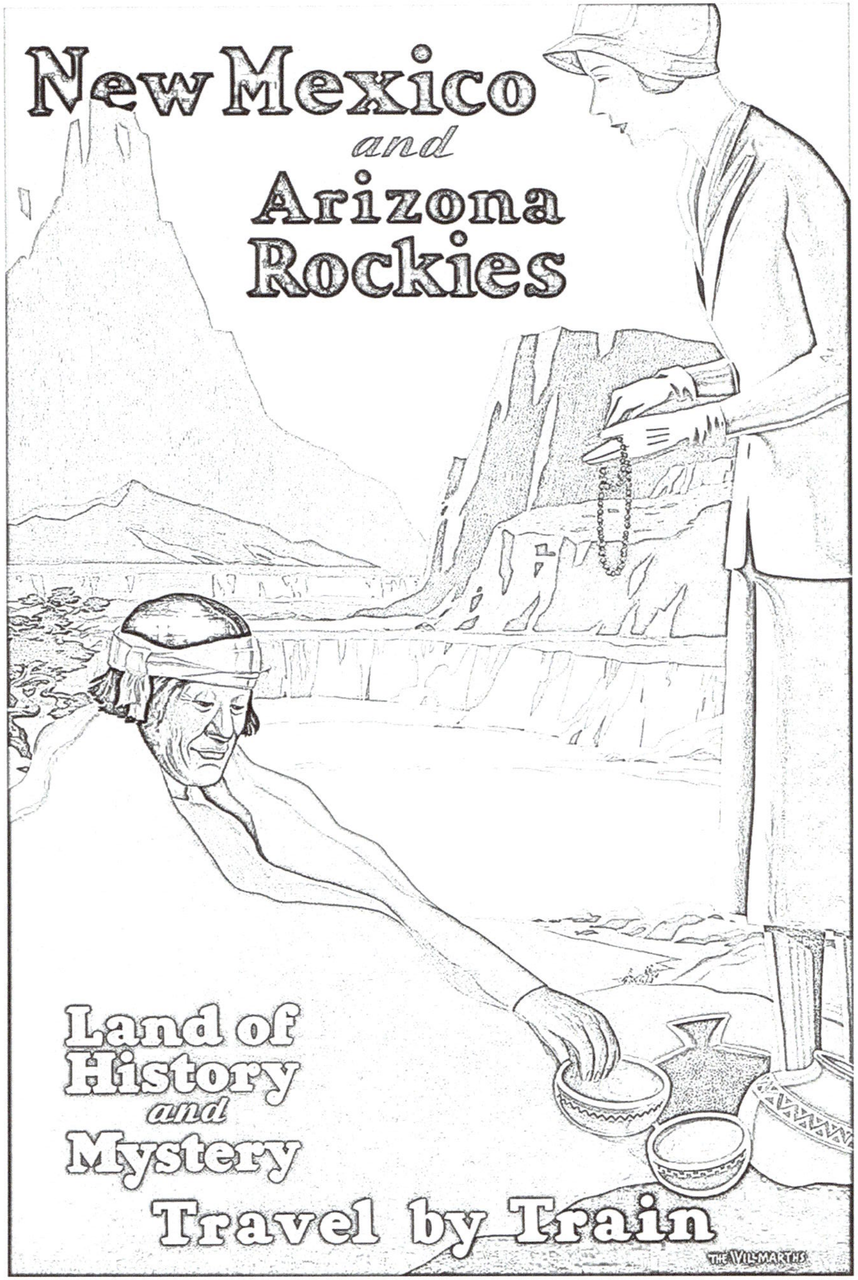
New Mexico
and
Arizona
Rockies
Land of
History
and
Mystery
Travel by Train
THE WILMARTHS

POST CARD

PLACE STAMP HERE

POST CARD

PLACE STAMP HERE

POST CARD

PLACE STAMP HERE

POST CARD

PLACE STAMP HERE

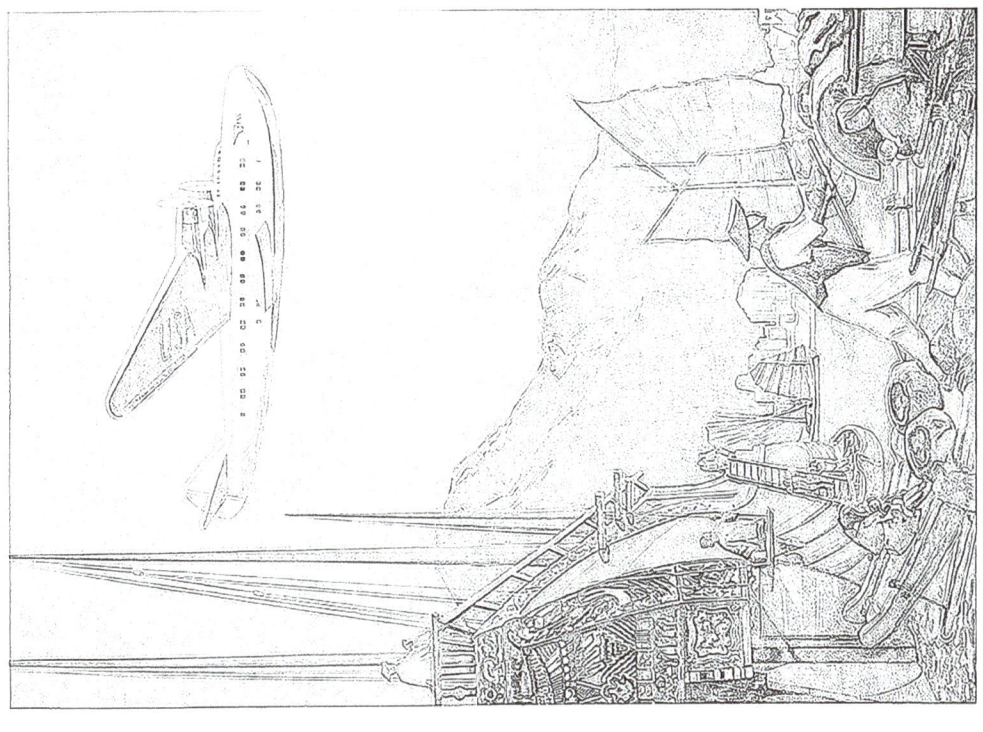

POST CARD

PLACE STAMP HERE

POST CARD

PLACE STAMP HERE

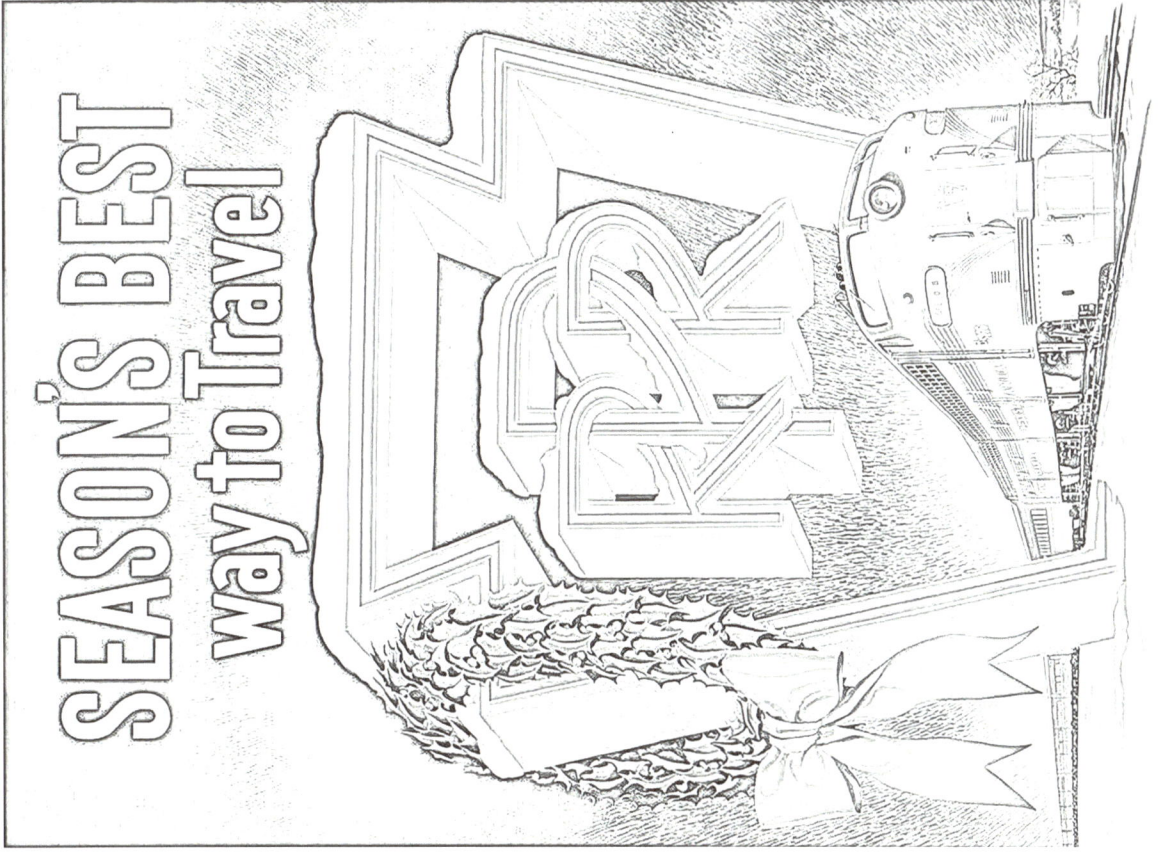

POST CARD

PLACE STAMP HERE

POST CARD

PLACE STAMP HERE

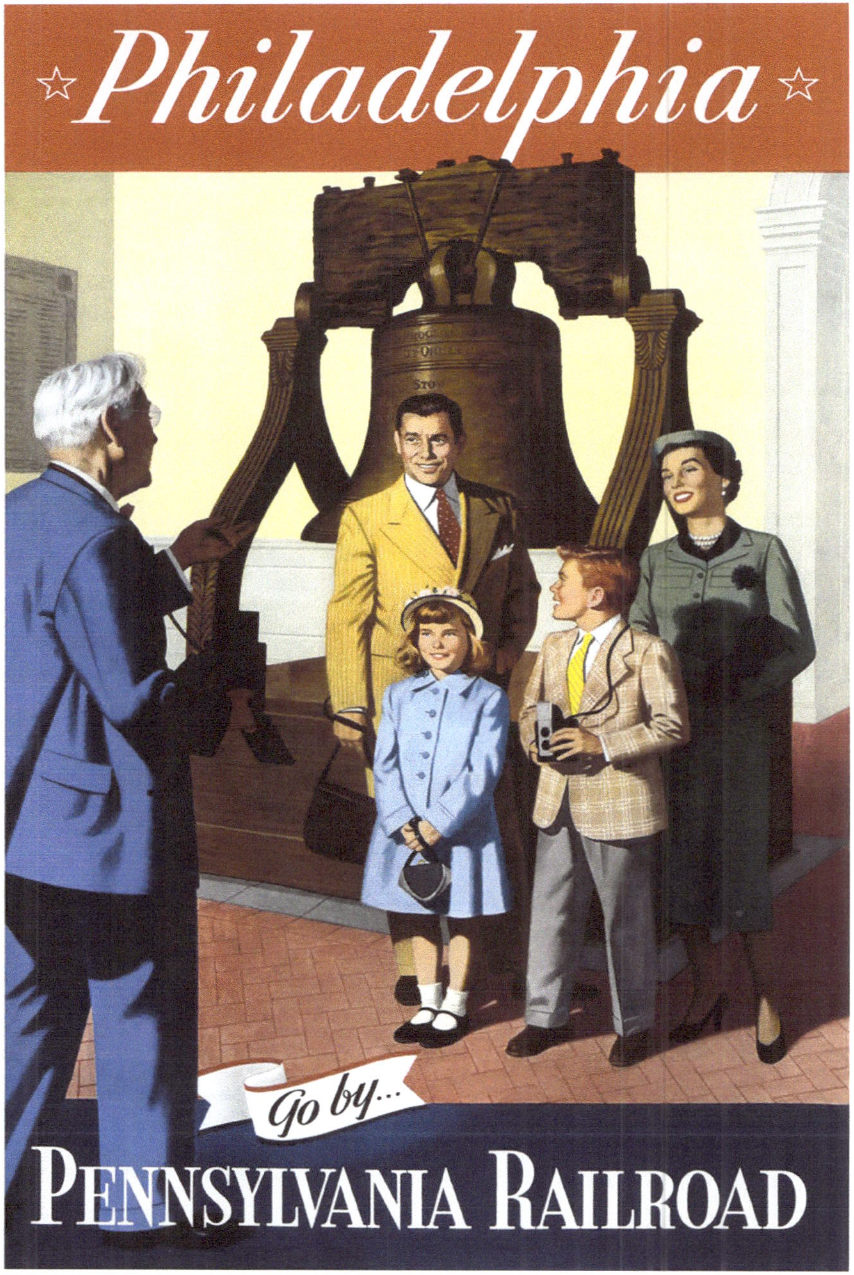
Philadelphia
Go by...
PENNSYLVANIA RAILROAD

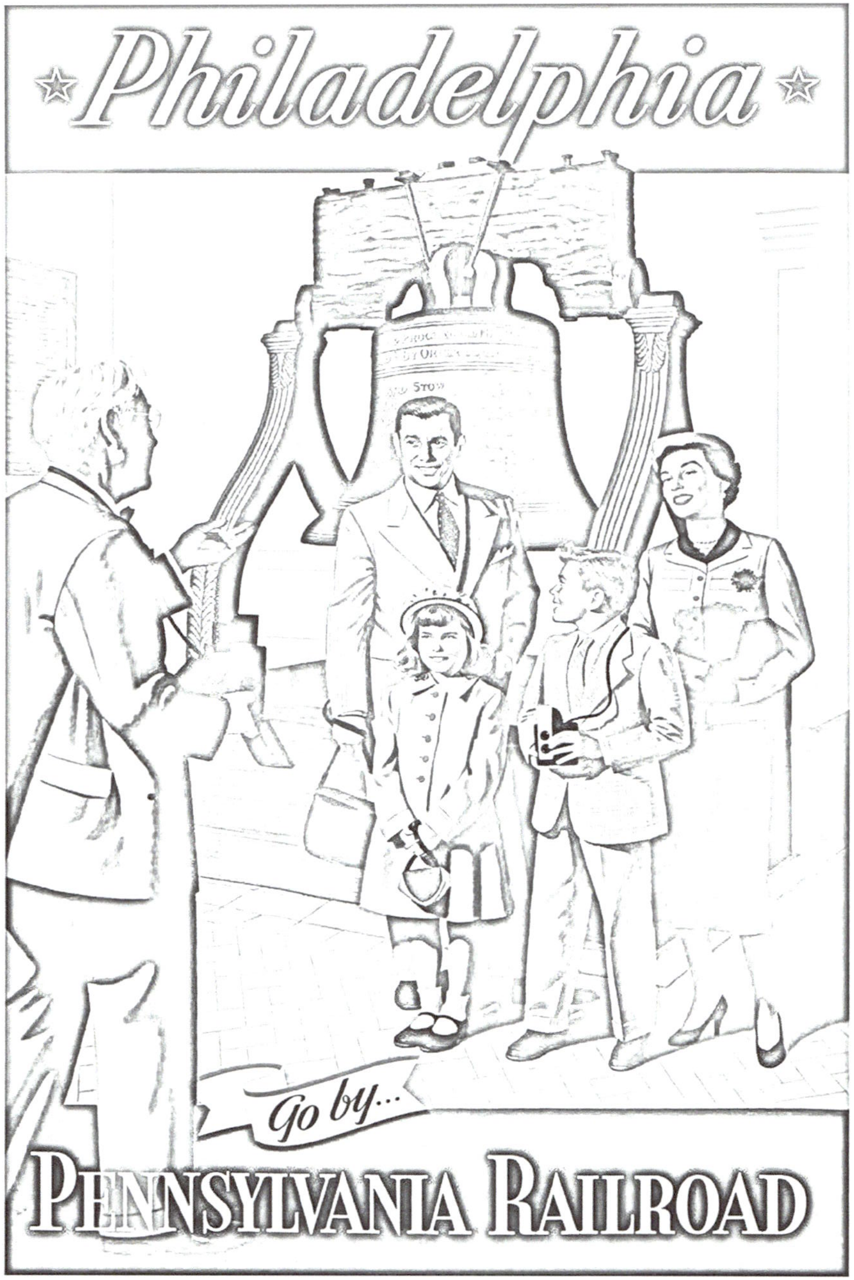
Philadelphia
Go by...
PENNSYLVANIA RAILROAD

POST CARD

PLACE STAMP HERE

POST CARD

PLACE STAMP HERE

POST CARD

PLACE STAMP HERE

POST CARD

PLACE STAMP HERE

POST CARD

PLACE STAMP HERE

POST CARD

PLACE STAMP HERE

POST CARD

PLACE STAMP HERE

POST CARD

PLACE STAMP HERE

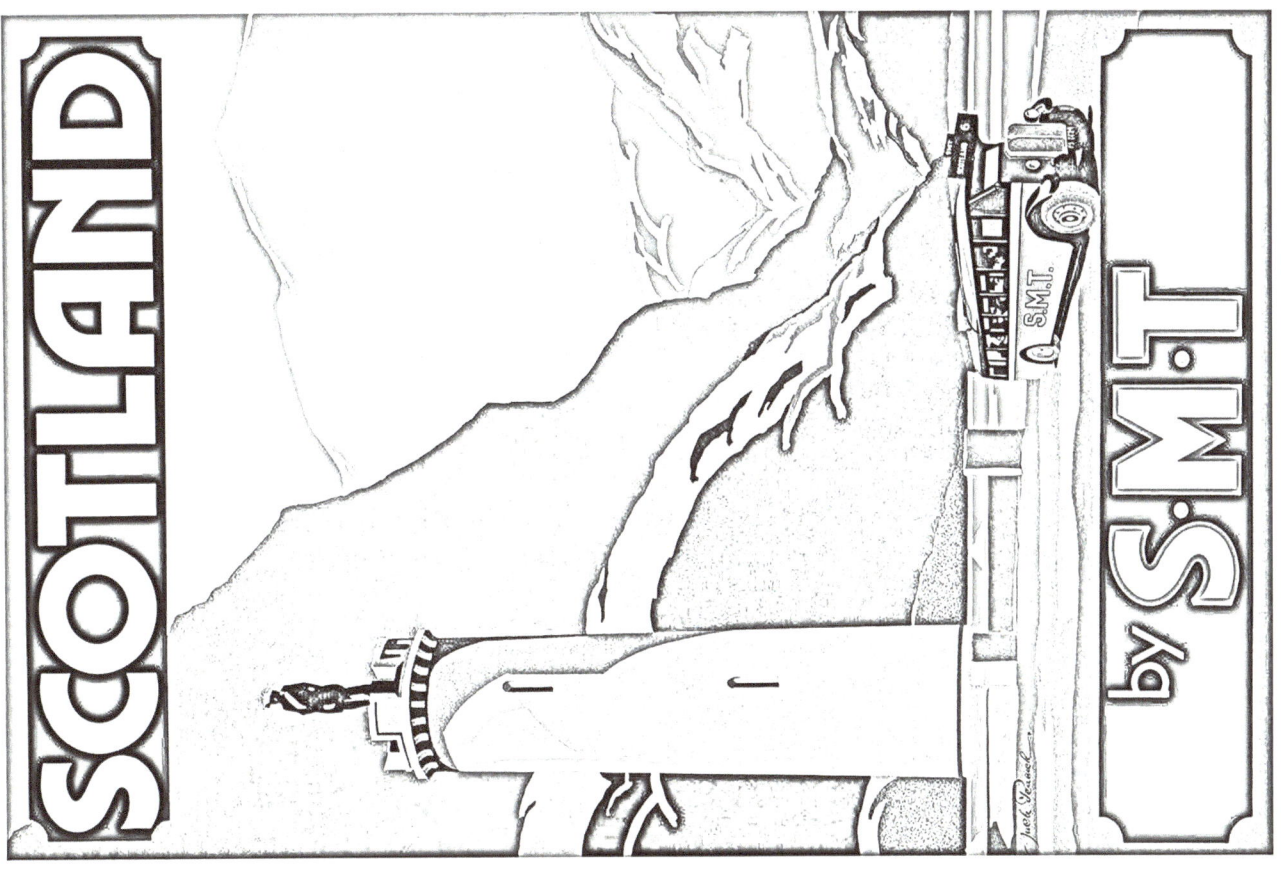

POST CARD

PLACE STAMP HERE

POST CARD

PLACE STAMP HERE

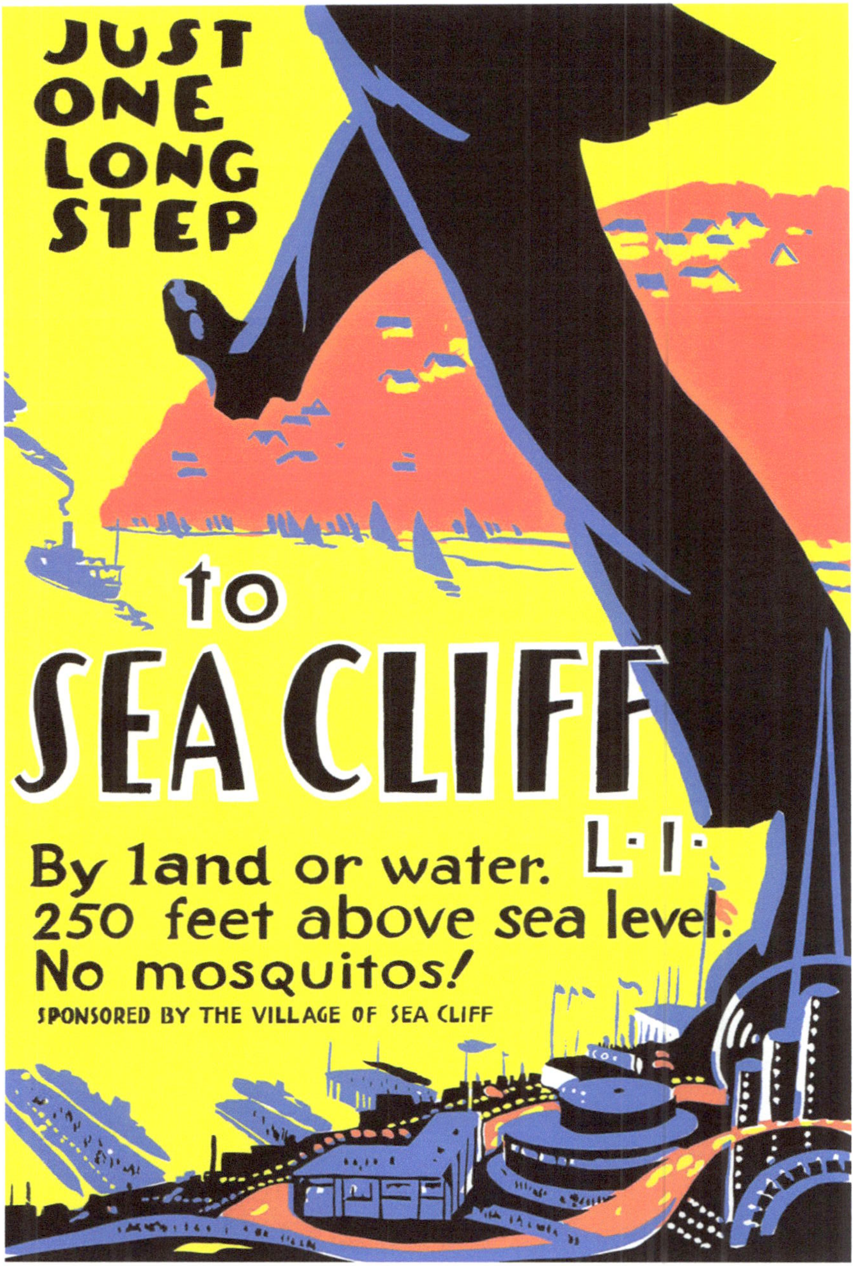
JUST
ONE
LONG
STEP
to
SEA CLIFF
L·I·
By land or water.
250 feet above sea level.
No mosquitos!
SPONSORED BY THE VILLAGE OF SEA CLIFF

JUST
ONE
LONG
STEP
to
SEA CLIFF
L·I·
By land or water.
250 feet above sea level.
No mosquitos!
SPONSORED BY THE VILLAGE OF SEA CLIFF

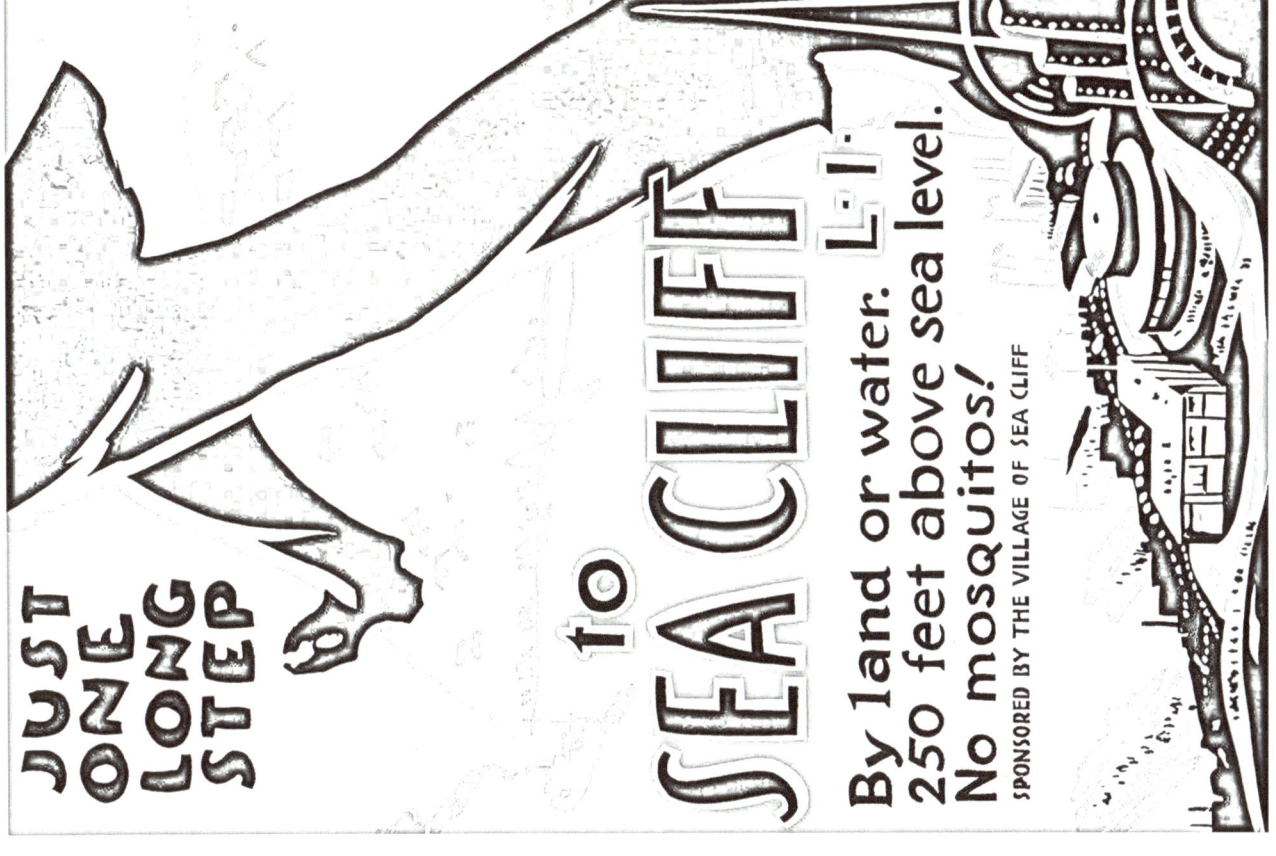

POST CARD

PLACE STAMP HERE

POST CARD

PLACE STAMP HERE

POST CARD

PLACE STAMP HERE

POST CARD

PLACE STAMP HERE

POST CARD

PLACE STAMP HERE

POST CARD

PLACE STAMP HERE

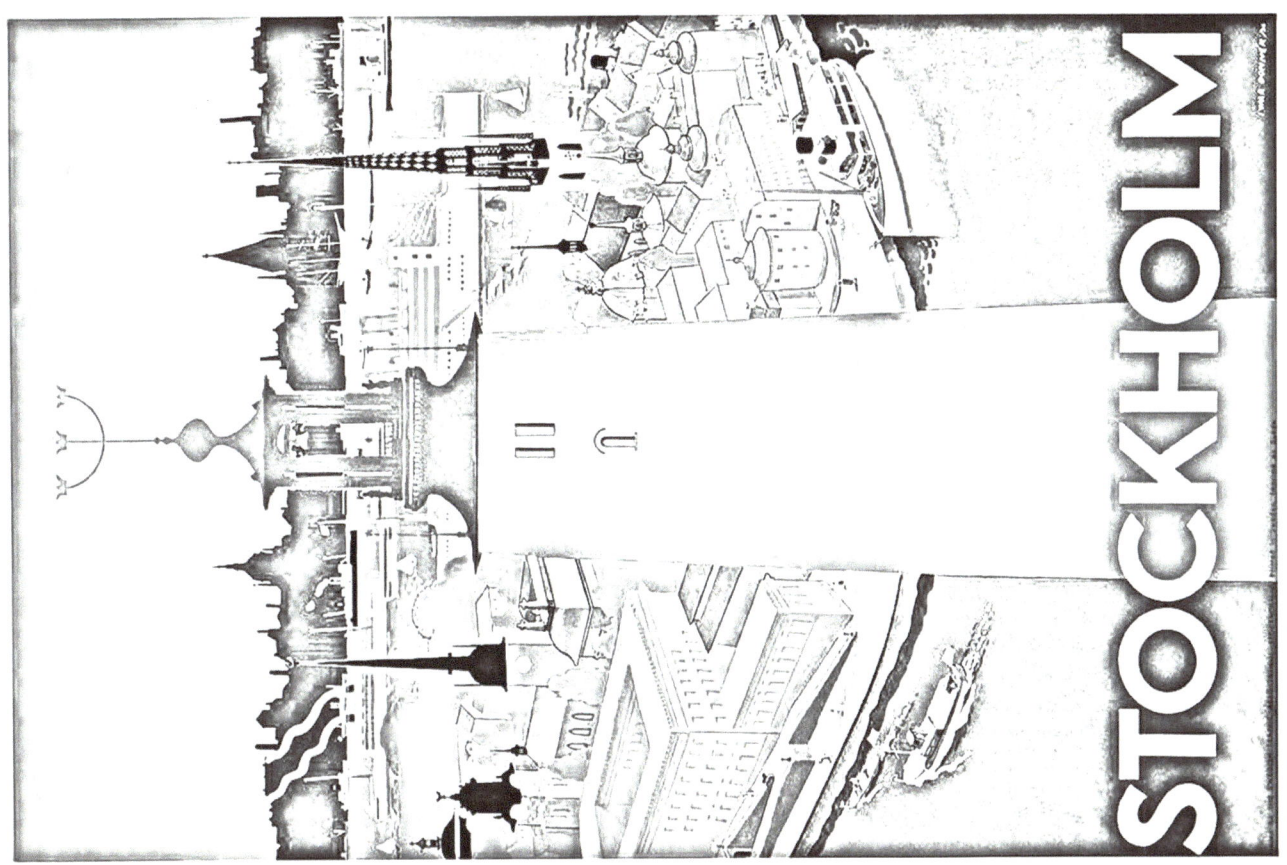

POST CARD

PLACE STAMP HERE

POST CARD

PLACE STAMP HERE

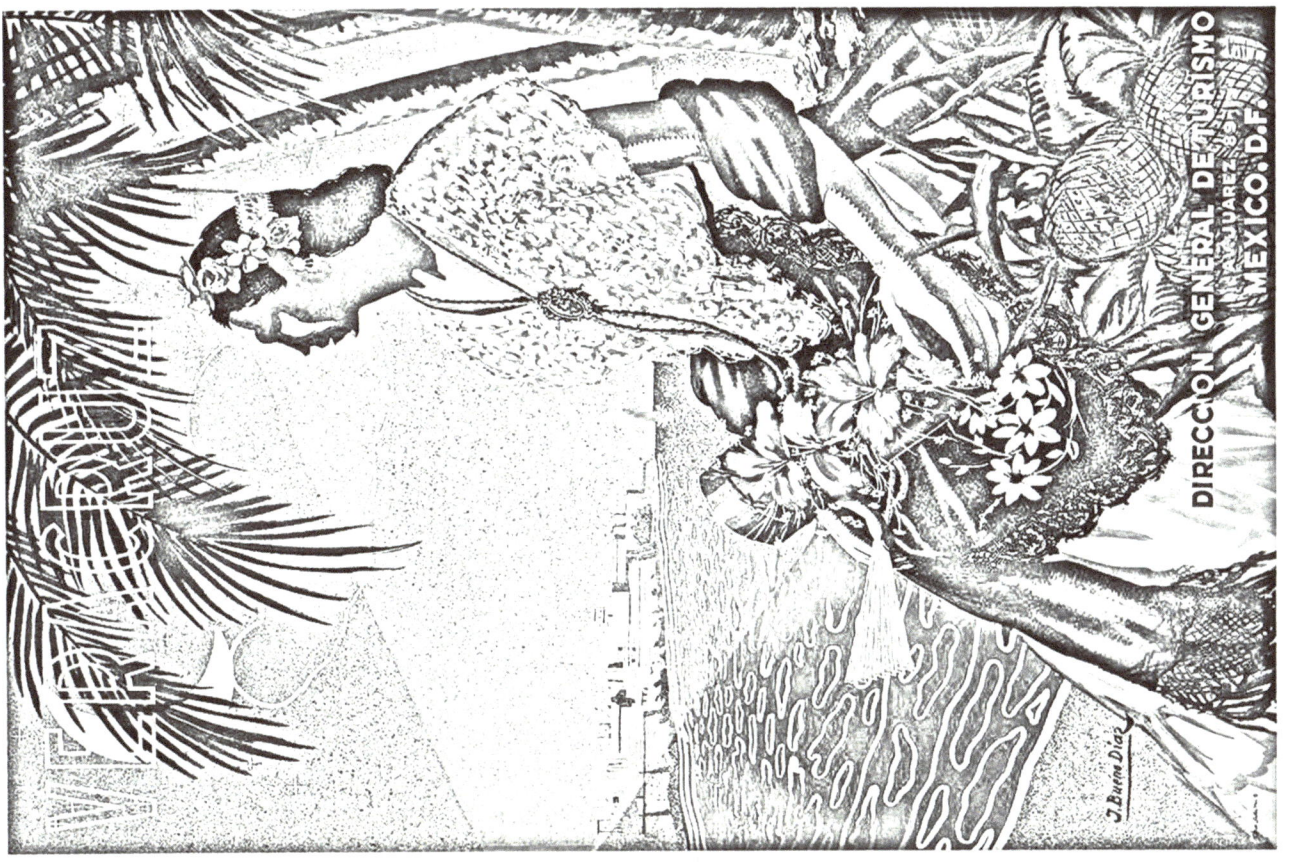

POST CARD

PLACE STAMP HERE

POST CARD

PLACE STAMP HERE

ENIT
VERONA

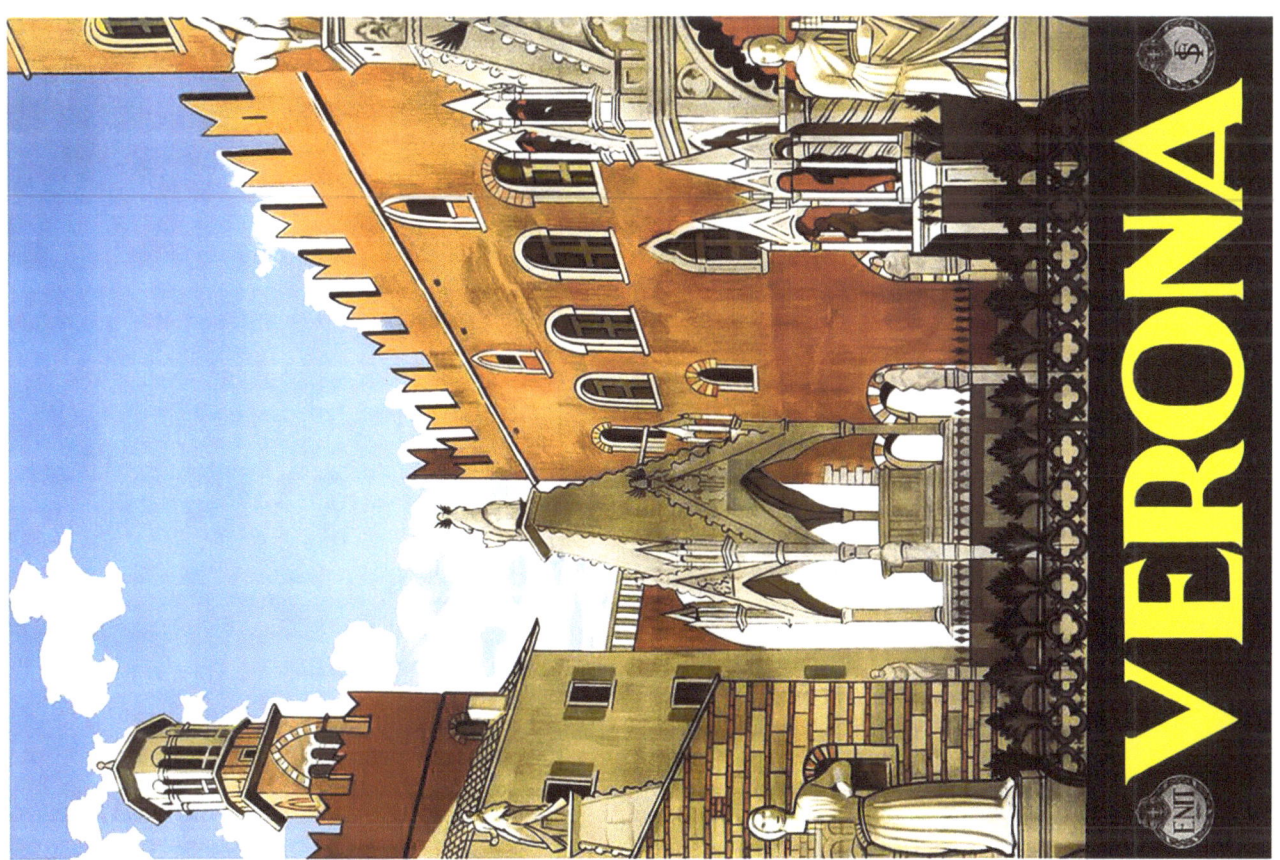

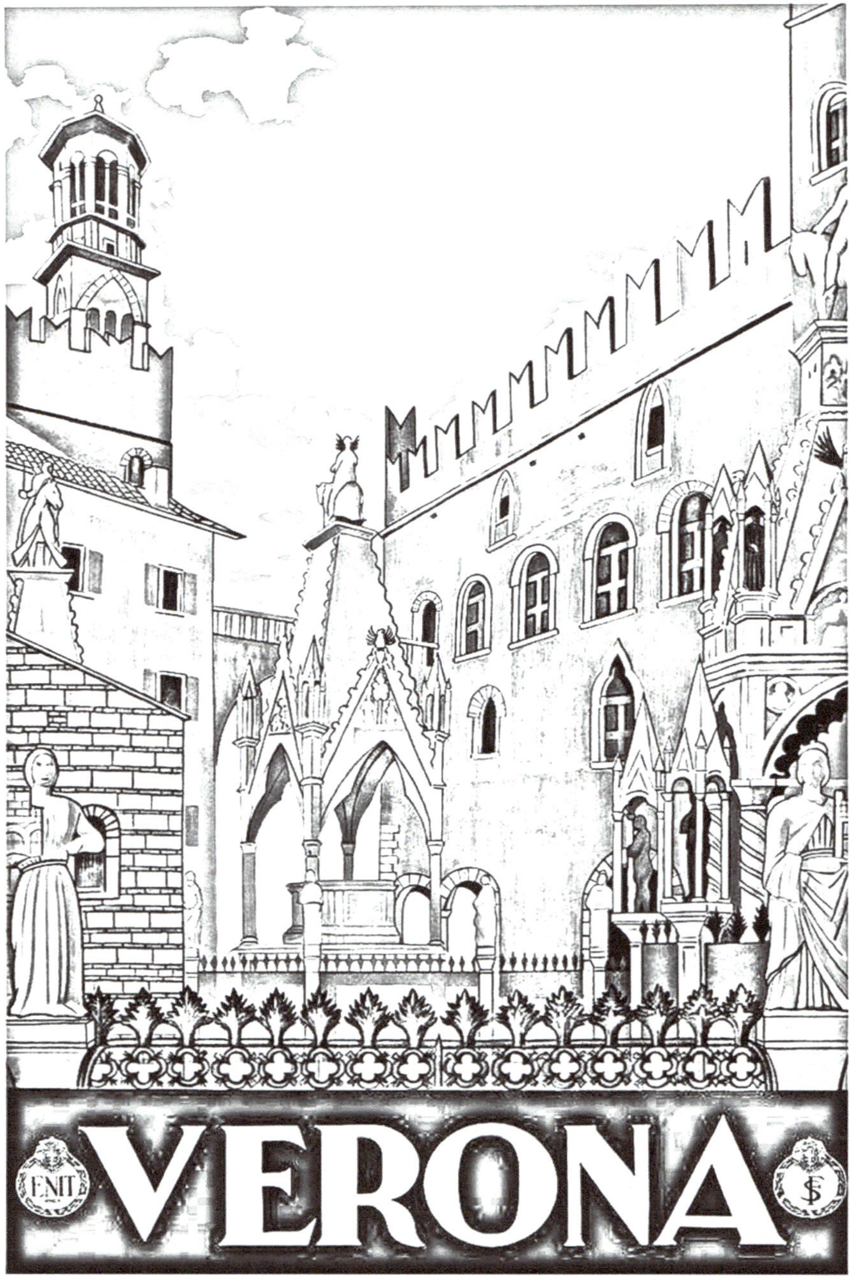
ENIT
VERONA

POST CARD

PLACE STAMP HERE

POST CARD

PLACE STAMP HERE

POST CARD

PLACE STAMP HERE

POST CARD

PLACE STAMP HERE

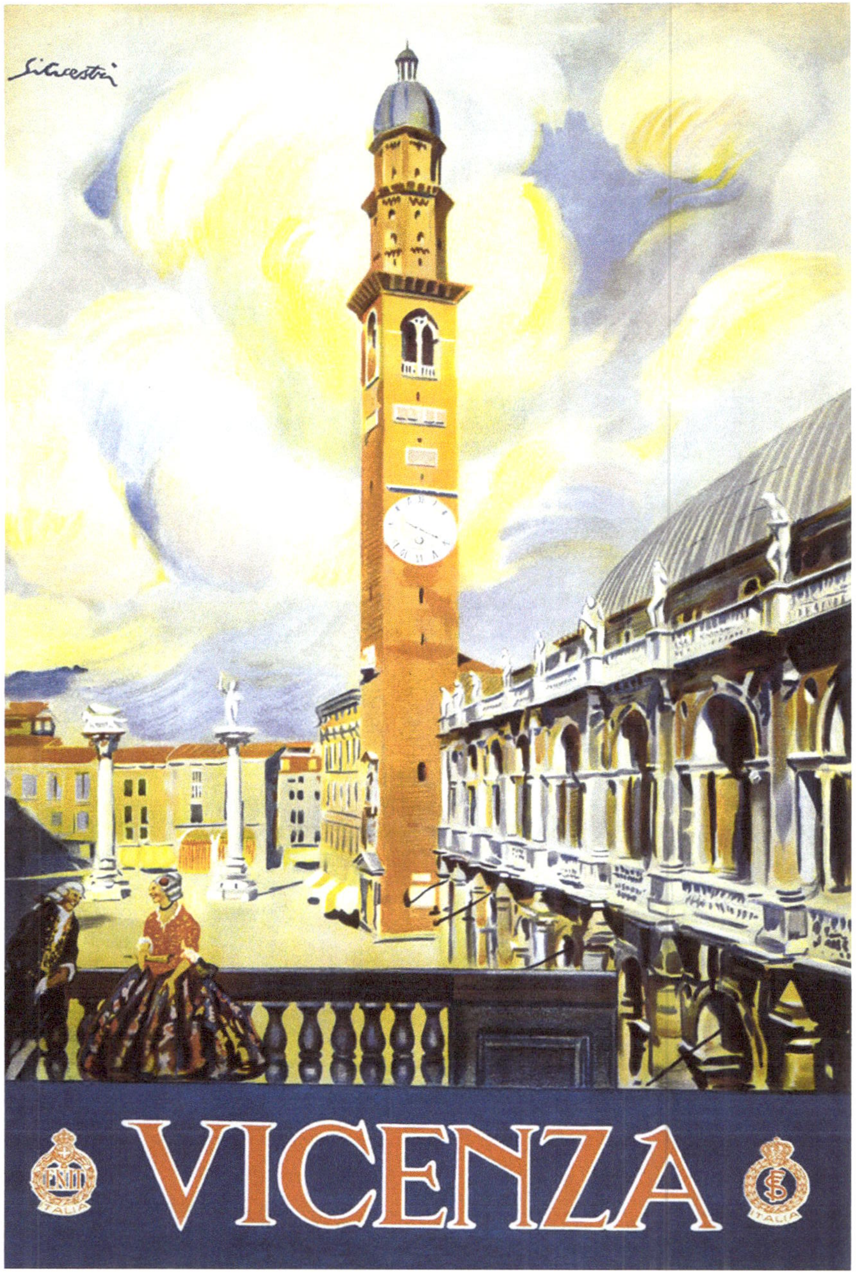

VICENZA

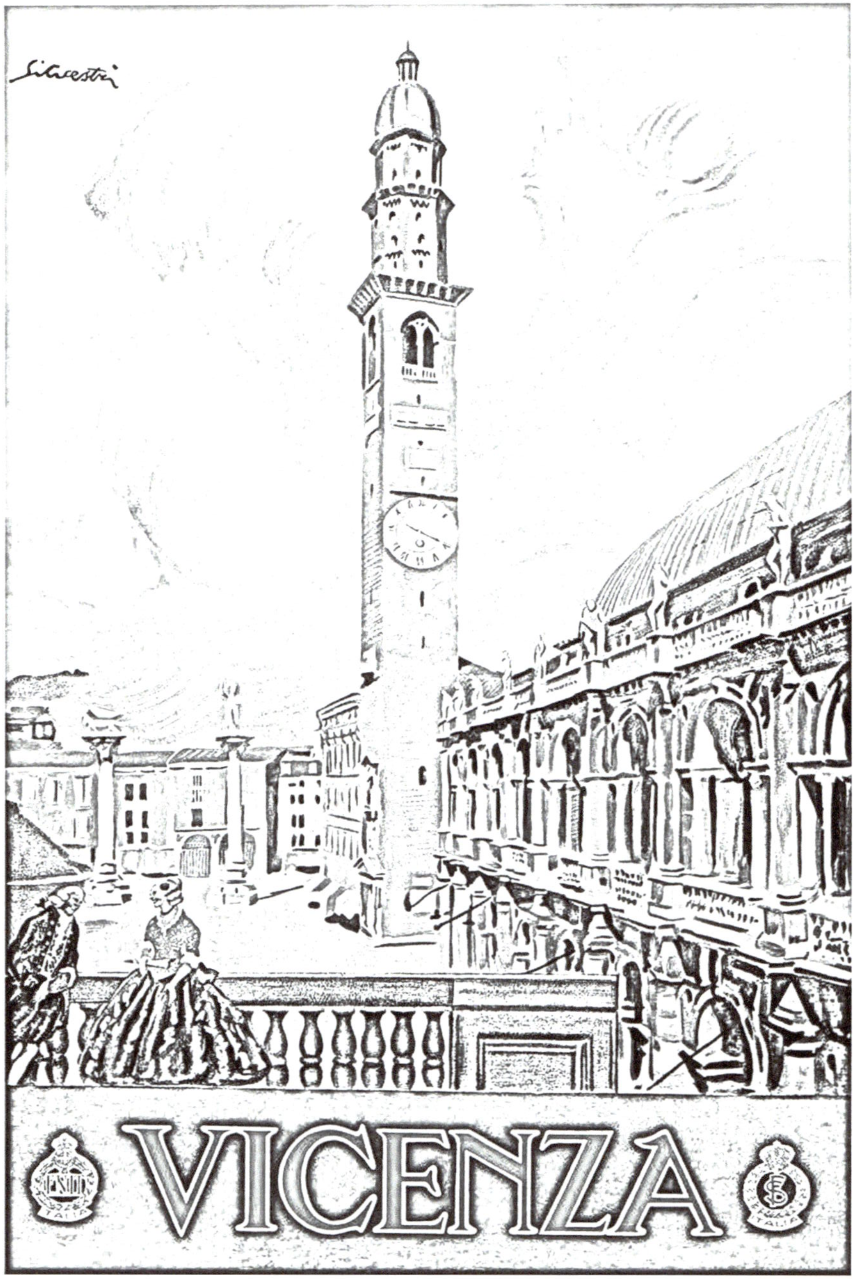

POST CARD

PLACE STAMP HERE

POST CARD

PLACE STAMP HERE

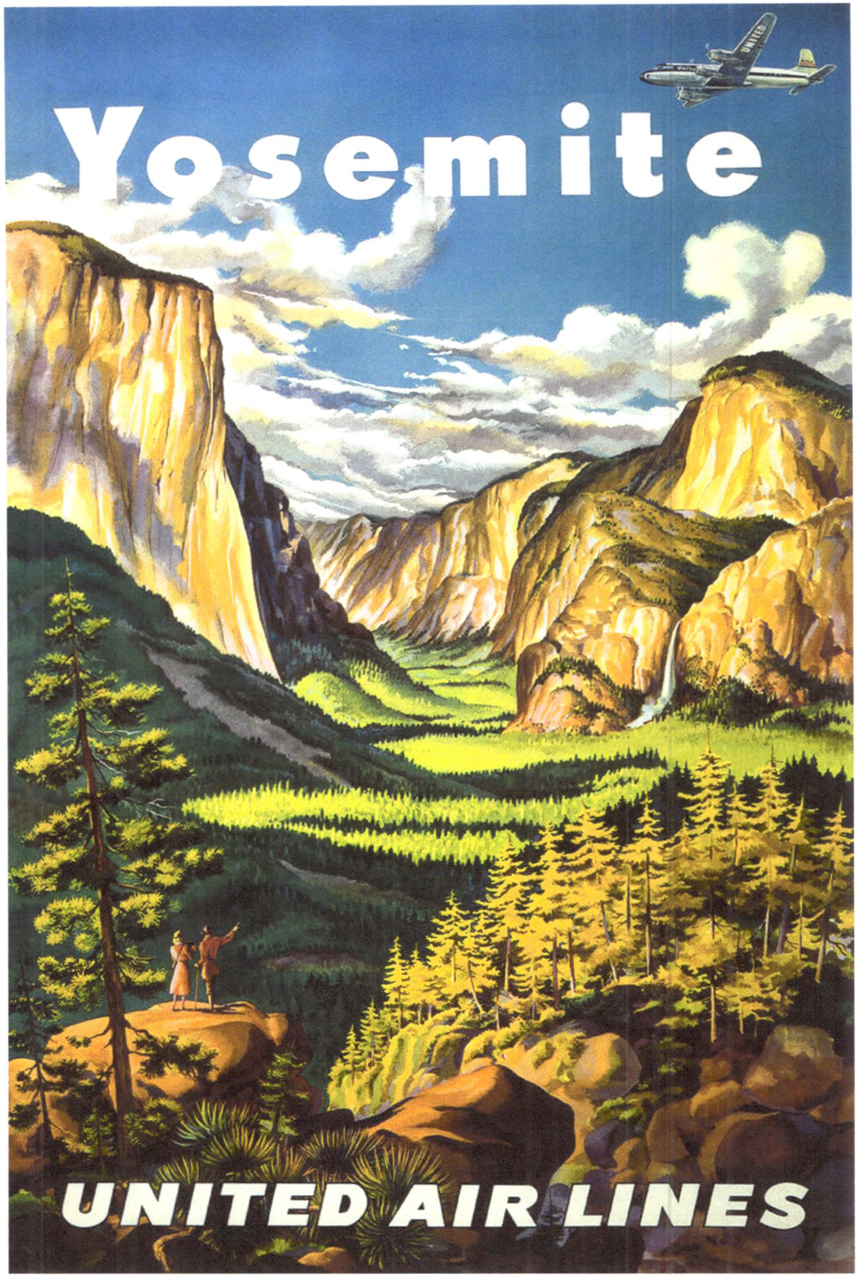
Yosemite
UNITED AIR LINES

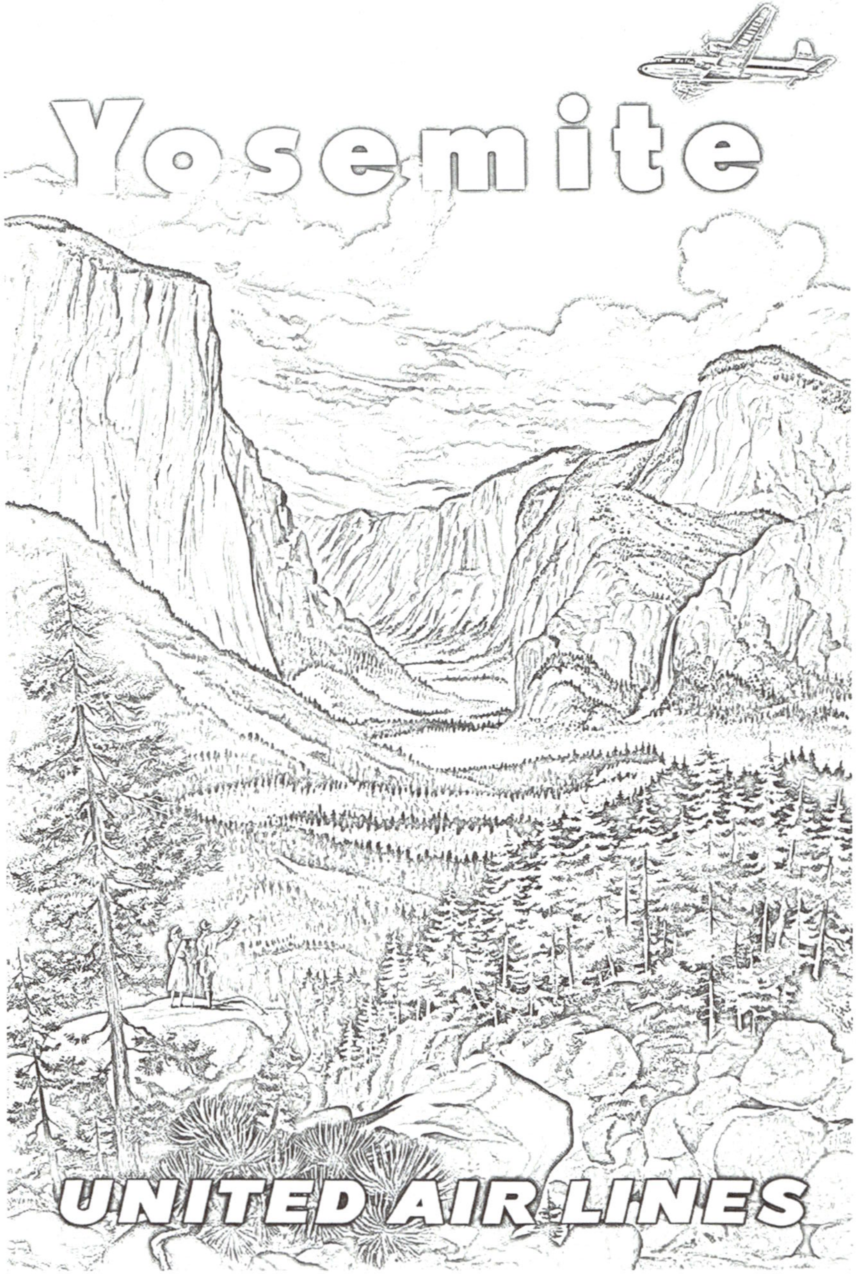
Yosemite
UNITED AIR LINES

POST CARD

PLACE STAMP HERE

POST CARD

PLACE STAMP HERE

HOW TO GET THE RESULTS YOU WANT VIDEOS:

Coloring these pages is easier than it looks, especially when you know a few tricks. Check out Jodie Randisi's Coloring Sanremo video.

https://youtu.be/_QPU7RK5ki0

TO SCHEDULE A COLORING WORKSHOP CONTACT:

jodie@coloringdepot.com.

EST. COWCATCHER 1992
PUBLICATIONS
HILTON HEAD, SC

This publication is available at a discount when purchased in quantity to use as a premium, sales promotion, in corporate training programs, or by schools or organizations for educational or cause marketing purposes.

CONTACT

(843) 816-7883
jodie@coloringdepot.com

www.ingramcontent.com/pod-product-compliance
Lightning Source LLC
Chambersburg PA
CBHW061402090426
42743CB00003B/119